Praise for the Author

Charlene weaves together current and historical data with her personal, spiritual, and emotional journey to wholeness as she sets the stage and captures the attention of readers with her new book, Building Resilience. She guides her readers into discovering some of the potentially destructive impacts of trauma, and how life-altering residuals can be substantially minimized by learning resilience. Charlene's book inspires hope with a step-by-step guide for building resilience. It's a must read!

In His Service,

— Dr. Mary G. Patton
www.drmarygpattonbooks.org

True resilience is defined by overcoming heartache, trauma, and negativity. Charlene Ransom not only helps people become more resilient through her counseling but has lived a life of resilience. Through her own challenging life experiences, education and putting in the work, she has developed a model & perspective on how to build a firm foundation to a life of resiliency.

— Dr. George James, CEO of George Talks, LLC
Licensed Marriage & Family Therapist, Media & Corporate Consultant, Speaker and Executive Coach.

In today's society, almost everyone has been impacted by a traumatic event whether directly or indirectly and I believe Charlene's book provides wonderful language from laypersons to students to professionals alike to shift their current conversations to becoming trauma informed conversations. Charlene challenges her readers to be intentional and informed about the impact of our interactions with people especially regarding those experiencing trauma. As she interweaves colorful stories about her own journey and many others that she has encountered throughout her life, we learn that what we do, don't do, say and don't say matters especially where trauma is concerned.

— Katrina N. Edmonds, LMFT
Be Set Free Counseling Ministry & Education Center

In Resilience The Ingredients of a Firm Foundation, Charlene takes readers on a journey through her life sharing the trauma she endured and how it played a role in shaping her identity and perspective. Readers will discover however that lining her path was a reservoir of resilience that empowered her to not only redefine her purpose but cultivate courage and spiritual growth. Charlene's raw honesty, humor and transparency provides a fresh approach to the idea of trauma and the effect it has on our total being. Ultimately Resilience will cause readers to discover and activate their own "bounce back" and power to overcome every setback, struggle or tragedy they will face.
BE EMPOWERED!

Niki Brown, Speaker | Coach | Author
Host of IGNITE Women's Empowerment Summit
www.ignitesummit.org
www.nikibrown.org

Resilience

Resilience

The Ingredients of a Firm Foundation

CHARLENE S. RANSOM

Resilience

Editor: k. Edward

ISBN: 978-1-7376022-3-1

Contents

Foreword

IN FULL DISCLOSURE, when Charlene asked me to write the foreword for her book, I had mixed emotions. First, I felt excitement and honor. What a privilege, I thought, to share in her journey with the world about overcoming trauma through building resiliency. That's my area of expertise. This will be easy. The second emotion was anxiety. Yep, I am a perfectionist and I tend to overthink and process a hundred times slower than many to get this perfect for her.

Charlene and I became acquainted through our work together at Bethany Baptist Church in the counseling ministry department, and subsequently continued to come into contact with one another through another powerhouse ministry leader, Reverend Niki Brown and the Ignite Women's Empowerment Conferences—and now Summit. Our paths continued to cross in many ways: Charlene and I share similar interests and opportunities. I have always appreciated her candor, forthrightness, and humor, and I expected nothing less in her narrative, *Resilience: The Ingredients of a Firm Foundation.*

In her personal narrative, Charlene Ransom has written the most compelling, thought-arousing and authentic narrative of the lived experiences of being a survivor of many of life's tragedies, from being a child survivor of child sexual abuse, exposure to parental, mental, and physical disabilities to teen parenting and family dysfunction. This narrative in the form of a first-person account is candid and relatable. Not only does she share her experiences, but she integrates clinically relevant vignettes and TIPS (trauma-informed point) to help the reader make connections between the triggering event and what the mental health professionals and theorists have learned about trauma theory, in an effort to avoid re-traumatizing readers while unpacking the pain of their past.

As I read parts of Charlene's story, I was reminded of the work of Dr. Faith C. Wokoma, psychologist and pastor who wrote, *Marked: Unraveling and Understanding the Call of God on Your Life (2018).* In sum, Dr. Wokoma teaches that the enemy can sense when there is something unique on your life and seeks to destroy you before you are born (p. 5). She further elaborates her statement that he may not take you out at birth but he will use life circumstances and challenges as attacks, such as a childhood marked with sickness, poverty, or abuse (p. 6) or emotional attacks, such as a mother who has suffered with anxiety and depression, which attach to you from the womb (p.7). I believe that, based on Charlene's authentic self-disclosures, the enemy had her marked at childhood. But too bad for the enemy, who may have had her marked, not to carry forth in her greatness, because God has a greater call for her life, and God triumphed! Because Charlene developed the ability to overcome adversity and build resiliency through her pain, we all win!

While this narrative may trigger some sadness and a revisiting of old wounds, I see this as an opportunity for healing. Charlene is sharing her story to set some of us free from the emotional wounding and baggage we have been carrying for years. Don't let this testimony fall on deaf ears or hardened hearts. Ms. Ransom exposes herself and her story with some emotional risk for you to see what is possible when you walk in your authenticity and truth. Healing is possible, but you must do your work.

For helpers, therapists and healers who are reading this narrative, it will be seminal in your work with emotionally wounded people who have layers of traumatic experiences that include race and ethnicity, gender, sex and age discrimination, disabilities, poorer social determinants of health, religion, etc. Her work reminds us as professionals about the humanistic perspective in working with persons who are working through difficult parts of their story to live lives without defeat! How you might ask: through a healthier life balance and developing coping skills that are in alignment with your vision, calling and mission to not permit trauma to define who we are.

Charlene, we are all grateful that you were obedient and followed the prompting of the Lord about the "right time" to put your story on to paper to share with the world. Your expertise in trauma-informed care, the impact of abuse on developing brains, and the capacity to develop resilience in spite of early challenges in your life, is a work that will benefit many students in the helping field, as well as our clients and seasoned professionals. I, too, hope that we will find some parts humorous, and that other parts will challenge our assumptions about trauma, and that we will find hope and encouragement as we seek to find our purpose in this life.

Gratefully Submitted to the Call,
Dr. Angela Clack, licensed psychotherapist, author, speaker
CEO, Clack Associates, LLC
www.clackassociates.com

Preface

CONFIDENCE. WRITING THIS book was the equivalent of completing a capstone project for my life. Surviving sexual abuse at the age of 10 and being told that I was not able to learn when I was in the seventh grade by my school guidance counselor are just two of the many challenges I'd faced. Being able to look back over my life and invite readers into my journey from a perspective that will help others overcome the trauma they may have experienced, as well as help those who may be working with others to better relate to, understand and support those with a trauma-informed perspective is the mission for this project.

Over the years, I've worked hard on my self-image, exchanging the lies told to me by others that I once believed, for truth. Viewing myself as unworthy, not smart enough, having a poor self-image and extremely low self-esteem was what I believed to be my truth. Seeing this same damaging and distorted image in many of the young people, and even adults, I was working with compelled me to write a book about my life from my genesis, through childhood abuse, my education years, and the many other experiences that should have canceled out my destiny. I learned to be what God said about me and use my past to define my future. My past has become the foundation for my purpose. God said "*That I am more than a conqueror!*" Through the many mistakes, failures and mishaps over the course of my self-discovery, God has protected and loved me. He has given me some amazing gifts in this life—friends and family who have loved and nurtured the broken piece of my life and have transformed me into the strong courageous woman I have become. Oftentimes I catch myself standing in front of my bathroom mirror dancing and smiling at the woman looking back at me, because for so many years I didn't love her.

Navigating the challenges of learning was hard, but I was able to do it nonetheless! Oh, I might have even failed a few tests but I was able to learn without any special accommodations from my professors. I never mentioned to any of my colleges that I had been classified as unable to learn when I was in the seventh grade. Please understand: I believe that in order that all children be taught and given an encouraging and safe place to learn, it is important that the style of learning for each child be considered and a responsible plan be created so the learning can take place. I graduated from high school, Bible college, community college, and from Rutgers University twice! I learned how to grow my strengths, and I received help with my weaknesses. And, despite what my parents were told, I could learn and I did; in fact, I mastered it.

Fluctuating from first-hand accounts, sharing information learned over the span of my life and through personal experience within the classroom it is my hope and prayer that the reader understands as I have: Every trial and tribulation that was meant to destroy my destiny has fueled my perseverance and desire to learn and become the person I am today. My determination to be a better person meant learning to see myself as God saw me. He created you and me in His image and likeness; we are the head and not the tail. Knowledge of this has pushed and propelled me to write and share how my life was mapped out long before I was a flicker in my parents' eyes. It tells just how all things the good and the very ugly worked together for my good according to God's purpose for my life. It is the providential nature of God that defines and solidified His plans in my life. Even when I didn't know him, He always had me covered in his love and favor.

Trauma, abuse, and resilience are subject matters that I've become an expert in, with intimate knowledge of them all. Bestselling author Malcolm Gladwell said that one can be considered an expert after spending 10,000 hours doing a particular thing. For example, to be a chess master you should play for a minimum of 10 years which totals to 87,600 hours to be considered an expert in chess. At the time this book was written, I calculated over 438,000 hours of experience in trauma, abuse, and resilience. Ok that settles it, I am definitely an EXPERT!

Discerning my time versus God's time to write this book was something I had to learn. I've found myself compelled to share my story; however, timing is everything. I wasn't mentally, emotionally, or even physically ready, so God kept saying that now was not the right time. For example, being emotionally bitter at my mother wasn't healthy, nor would it have been useful in helping others, nor struggling with my worth as a person, nor doubting my ability to be a good parent to my son. God was saying I needed to resolve those issues before telling someone else that they can overcome issues in order to become mentally healthy.

Eventually, after working with a therapist for many years, attending support groups, lots of prayer and trusting God's promises found in His word, I am able to discern those who had harmed me intentionally versus those who have passively harmed me. Neither felt good, but learning how others have their own trauma history was paramount in my ability to forgive, understand others, exchange the lies I believed about myself, and become able to develop confidence in myself, as well as becoming able to see me as God sees me: the apple of His eye.

Now it is my prayer that as you read Resilience, you do not focus solely on the negative crap, like having my armpits scrubbed with a copper-tip scrub brush because my hormones and sweat glands produced earlier than most children. When I was four or five I had to wear deodorant because I had an underarm odor. Later I learned that because of the various drugs my mother had to take when she went through her cancer treatments, it could have caused my hormones to develop sooner than the average child my age. Nor is it my intention to shame my family or bring attention to the dysfunction that is common in many families. We all have that one family member who we hate to see coming to the family BBQ because we knew after just a few drinks of "spirits" they want to fight any and every one. I know you just thought of that one person, didn't you?

Constructed in a manner that enables the reader to glean a better understanding of complex trauma and how it impacts the family, Resilience can be a useful tool. As a therapist, teacher, or just a layperson, you will have a better understanding of the way it impacts the individual, relationships, community, and society.

Evidence of God's love and plans for me was shown before my birth. He favored me when He chose that my passage into this world would be through the womb of an amazingly confident and strong woman. God in His all-knowing self, knew she was the perfect person to pick for the task of assuring my arrival into this world. She was a fighter and overcomer who was determined to not be defeated by the challenges she faced in life. Her will and courage is the reason why I'm strong willed, compassionate, patient, empathetic, and spend my life advocating for those who can't fight for themselves.

Within these pages, I share some very intimate stories; some are funny, some not so funny, but each with a trauma-informed clinical perspective. They each belong to me and I own each one as a badge of honor to the courageous and resilient person I have become. This book is the reward for my survival of it all. What I celebrate and hope you're able to glean from this book is the hope, courage, and grace to discover the purpose of your life. No matter what you have experienced, you are still here, and purpose is waiting for you to begin to walk in it. Be inspired and motivated to give back to those you choose to serve in the community. After all, you too have the ingredients to be resilient.

Introduction

per·so·na
/ˌpərˈsōnə/

A persona is an image or personality that a person presents in public or in a specific setting —as opposed to their true self.

INSPIRED. IF I can be frank—of course, I can, it's my book, right? For many years I didn't know who I was, nor did I understand my purpose for living. In fact, because I had no idea that my life had a purpose, I didn't portray myself as being someone else. I wasn't pretending to be some big shot, or live the facade of having more than I actually did. You know the "fake it to you make it' concept. I was always my authentic self; I have always considered the feelings and thoughts of others over myself. Being a caretaker for my parents, and providing for my son was all I knew how to do. I wasn't focused on my looks or driving the big fancy car. I just wanted to be able to provide a positive and safe place for myself and son to grow and become who God intended. Parenting him the way I wished my childhood was, was my only desire.

Nevertheless, knowing that I wasn't smart enough (because that's what the guidance counselor said), I didn't totally mind that I failed in college when I first went, right after high school. I wanted to prove those who said I couldn't succeed wrong. But the pressure of learning was too much for me and I really didn't know how to be a college student. I never learned how to study, or took a single class that could have prepared me for the basics of college life. Since I was classified as a special education student and diagnosed as unable to learn, I wasn't given the tools to succeed while I was in high school. I guess since there was no expectation of my future success; the school system felt I wasn't worth the investment, which is why I probably didn't make the investment in myself.

I never considered myself "pretty" because I was never told that I was. My mother usually referred to me as "High Yellow Bitch" or "Yellow Muther Fucker". Whereas my dad, who was my first best friend, called me "his boy," which was a compliment I loved to hear. I was proud to be his boy. That was our thing, I was his boy, the one who didn't cry over the little things like falling off my bike and busting up my knees. I was a daddy's girl who tagged along as my dad ran the Boy Scout Troop at one of the churches in our neighborhood. We went to every parade and all the Pinewood Derbies, and made racing cars together. Living with two boys growing up made me tough. I fought almost every single day during the school year. Plus, two of my brothers, Charlie and Marvin, would tell their bullies they would *sick* their sister on them. Marvin would summon me to the front porch with a frantic hand ocarina. I could be sitting in the living room, minding my business and out of nowhere a loud piercing sound would fill the air as Marvin ran for his life, desperately needing to get to his base, me. After hearing the call, I would answer, meeting both Marvin and my opponent in the front yard to hold court.

Prim and proper was not me at all, nor was I one for frills and lace. I hated dresses and would have preferred to look more like a boy; I had the hair for it. Dark brown frizz crowned my head and made me feel more like a boy until my mother decided she would press and curl it. Boy, did I dread those days. Some can relate to the fear of the hot comb and its slow and steady approach to the temple from a certified home beautician, which my mother was. However, she was also an amputee, which meant we both got to sit; I would be seated on an old wooden skate box, my butt numb. My mother would be seated at the kitchen table, with all the tools needed to fry my hair within arm's reach. Those presses lasted about two days if she was lucky. Sometimes she opted to braid my hair, which I hated. Her fingers could grip up the shortest of hairs. Botox had nothing on the facelift you got just from a cornrow by the one and only Mrs. Leola! About a day or two afterwards red bumps would strategically appear across the back of my neck as retribution for the style I wore. As much as I hated my mother doing my hair, having it done was everything. Sometimes, some of the older girls in my neighborhood, or my cousin Linda would do my hair when she came to visit; they gave me cute styles. I knew they were cute when the neighborhood said so.

Dresses were a constant reminder of what it was like to be a girl. A girl with boobies. I hated boobies. Men squeezed boobies and I didn't want to be squeezed. Finding myself less likely to be the center of attention if my breasts were hidden I opted for oversized anything. While writing, I have realized that oversizing is still something I struggle with today.

TIP The coping mechanism served me well as a child but as an adult I still find myself hiding my body in shame because I still struggle with the distorted view of this body that attracted the lust and lure of men twice my age and some three-to-four times older.

I think I might have triggered another childhood trauma just thinking about that hot comb. I had to be careful to hold my ear when my mother attempted to get every single hair pressed bone straight; the sizzling sound from the thumb touching greased hair would be the first warning to the possibility of your ear or forehead being burned by a slight touch of the comb. Not to mention she would knock me upside my head if I didn't hold it the right way. If my younger brother, Marvin, came and told her something I might have done to him she would pull my hair as a punishment.

According to a report from my Uncle MC—who was actually one of my parents' friends—I was really skinny, and for a few years my mother was told by our family doctor I was undernourished. A high yellow skin tone, with green veins you could see in my face, made nothing about my appearance beautiful to me. No one referred to me or talked about those features in a positive way; it was always in a negative. By the time I was 10, my breasts had grown beyond the standard training bra that most girls my age wore, making me hate my body more than anything. Boys my age would tease me and call me names; the older men only wanted to hug and squeeze them. When I looked in the mirror I saw this sad little girl who wished she could transform into someone who looked like Tootie from the television sitcom The Facts of Life, and become someone people noticed as being smart, pretty, and funny. Unlike Tootie, I didn't attend a fancy private school, or have rich parents who were lawyers or doctors; they did the best they could with what they had.

Don't get me wrong, like every young child, I too had dreams—or should I say plans to escape the horror of my childhood—when I grew up. I planned to enlist in the military after finishing high school to defend our country and make an impact in this world. I had grand plans to move to Germany and start my own accounting firm because the one thing I was good at was the 1040 EZ form. I wanted to become rich and successful as an entrepreneur. The plan was to buy a shiny, beautiful, black Mercedes Benz with a cream leather interior. Then, when I retired, I would move to Bermuda and live the beach bum life, sipping on cocktails as I planted my toes deep down in the sand. My perfect plan for my final years of living. If you want God to laugh, tell Him your plans, because He has something else in mind.

I graduated from high school, and left for college that summer. unbeknownst to anyone, I was three months pregnant when I graduated high school. No one knew but me and God. This is where I should mention some aspect of my relationship with God, like He's always been there for me even when no one else was. Despite being pregnant, I attended Cheyney University and majored in accounting. I started the summer program to gain some skills to be more prepared for college, but it was not enough. I struggled to keep up with my classes, along with morning sickness, always being tired and drained. I was placed on probation and ultimately suspended for having a very low GPA. I dropped out of college by maybe the fourth semester. When I had to return home, I was so disappointed in myself. I wanted to succeed just to prove my mother wrong. Instead, I was right back in my mother's house.

I was now with a child and basically, she was the de facto mother to my son and me. I was 19 years old, a single parent and stuck in my childhood home. I hated being there and worked all kinds of jobs so that eventually I was able to move out. Nothing seemed to match the plans I had for my life, but that didn't stop me from trying even harder. If one door closed, I went knocking on the next.

With my new-found adulthood came responsibilities that were greater than my teenage-mother brain could handle. For the life of me I don't know how folks are expected to maintain any quality of life, making minimum wage and kudos to those who are bringing home the bacon and frying it in the pan, because I couldn't. While working for minimum wage I managed to provide for my newborn son. I got evicted and had my car repossessed several times; that's what minimum wage did for me. Sure, I expected it to be difficult but who knew that it would be tedious and downright hard to find employment with just a high school diploma. My life just seemed to be a predictable cycle of what I wanted to prove to my mother as not being my outcome. She'd insisted that my life was going to be hard because I had a son and no husband to support us. Constantly she would remind me of how I would never amount to much because I had got pregnant before finishing college. Mrs. Leola said over and over again that I would amount to nothing; just having baby after baby and having no husband was what she predicted for my life.

The impact of the trauma and abuse that I endured over the years helped to negatively shape my view of self, my mother, and the world. I was unaware of my worth and felt in some small way defeated, and that she'd won. Not that there ever was a competition, but Mrs. Leola made living so hard. It was a task to get through the hours of the day without being verbally abused and belittled by her. However, the seeds of courage and determination to achieve more were planted and watered by the people God placed in my life. From the professionals who supported our family because of my parents' disabilities, to the nurturing women who showed me what it was to be a young lady, including my childhood friend's mother, Mrs. Barb. Women like Shirley, who lived just two doors away from me, were like big sisters. But more of a protector and nurturer, Shirley showed me how to love God and see myself as God saw me. Having respect for yourself was always a topic of discussion with Mrs. Bradley, who was also my mother's social worker. She was also the mother of Chris, the man who molested me. She taught me how to use my skills as a public speaker to address our local commissioners in order to get funding for a school trip when I was in high school. She, along with those mentioned, provided an example of what life could be.

I was a mother now and needed to know how to be one, whatever that meant. My girlfriends' mothers loved me for who I was, and I will forever be grateful for the examples of care and support shown to their daughters, as that was the model I needed in order to be the mother I desired. I listened to how respectfully they spoke to their daughters and took notes on how to never use derogatory name[s] when speaking to my child. Thank you to Lisa, Carolyn, Mae, Cathy and Terri for sharing your mothers with me. On many occasions, I secretly wished that they were mine. It was like their mothers provided a blueprint, and I wanted to model what I saw in each of them: respect and unconditional love.

Despite my environment, the trauma and many disadvantages, God's grace was present in every phase of my life; from teachers to social workers, to surrogate mother figures, I learned that I had the potential to do more, to be more, and nothing could stop me but myself.

re·sil·ient
/rəˈzilyənt/

According to The American Psychological Association, psychologists define resilience as the process of adapting well in the face of adversity, trauma, tragedy, threats, or significant sources of stress—such as family and relationship problems, serious health problems, or workplace and financial stressors. As much as resilience involves "bouncing back" from these difficult experiences, it can also result in profound personal growth. It was personal growth that prompted observers to string together phrases like "*bounce back kid*" to describe my transformation and response to adversity. My tenacity according to Rev. Sandra Coleman could only be compared to that of a *dog on a pant leg*; "You never give up," she'd say on occasion. And, for a long time in my head that was the title of the book I'd yet to write. Reverend Coleman was a sister-friend, a mentor and ministry leader. It was her structure and discipline that made serving under her easy. Losing focus when there is no order comes easy for me; however, Reverend Colman's model helped to keep me on track.

I loved her thirst and passion for the word of God. And I was certain He used her to speak life into me when I needed it most. One year, Rev. Colman invited me to go with her to a John Maxwell conference in Texas. John Maxwell was an author that I had admired and respected for some time; I had several of his books on leadership. He has a way of conveying a message that is easy to follow and comprehend. At the time I was a big fan of his and had several of his books. Overall, the trip was great. The time we spent together allowed us to create the foundation of what had developed into a mentor; a type of spiritual mother. Our friendship was one that drew me closer to God. Reverend Coleman was a leadership mentor who gave me the opportunity to serve in a leadership role when others within the church wouldn't. Her commitment to my spiritual development spoke to the bond of holy friendship, similar to that of Elija and Elisha, *2 Kings 2*.

The night before our flight home from the conference, I packed and got everything ready. We had to return a rental car prior to our flight, so I allotted time for that in our schedule. I'm not certain what happened, but something went amiss, literally—because we *missed* our flight. Realizing we'd approached crunch time mid-way through our airport quick-walk we switched gears and proceeded in O.J. mode—or at least Reverend Coleman did. A much heavier me had begun to sputter out. The disappointment in her face tore through my soul, and I knew I'd failed her in the worst way—so much so that I would believe be deposed from my position in the Sunday School Department. Unbeknownst to me I allowed my actions and previous experience of alleged failure to dictate how I would process Reverend Coleman's response before she'd even said a word. I automatically assumed she was going to terminate our relationship!

Fortunately, Reverend Coleman had a unique way of meeting me where I was. I would complete a task or assignment she had given and usually would undermine myself because I automatically thought it wasn't good enough or what she wanted. It was as if I saw my worth through the eyes of others' approval. But, she always saw the good in my service and had a unique way of making me see it as good. And in her words, *just accept the compliment and don't dismiss it with a negative thought*. It was as if she was God-assigned, and He used her that day to identify years of self-sabotaging behavior. Standing before her in shame and guilt was a shell of a Charlene standing in younger Charlene's run-down Converses. I waited for the verbal lashing like I waited for Mrs. Leola's hands. But that didn't happen, instead Reverend Coleman began with empathy: *"Get it together." Her eyes said she knew my struggle and understood what I needed. "Oh girl," her voice stern yet affirming, "You think when you mess up that others will reject you. You can't keep telling yourself that. Plus, that's not how God works."* A true friend will cover or bless you with a kind rebuke when needed. *Proverbs 28:23*

It wasn't easy, but I heard every word she said to me that day. I digested it. I thought about times before when I had felt that I would be given up on, or rejected; the difference was, as she explained to me: "You are not your failures." Be accountable for your failures or mistakes, learn from them and move on. No one had shown me that kind of grace before. I had never been told that I wasn't my mistakes or failures; as a result I had allowed them to define me. Reverend Coleman helped me to realize that others could not define me. It's God's plan that we be renewed in our thinking. As we are transformed in our mind, we begin to see and live out the perfect plan and will of God. I pride myself on not giving up when I don't understand the assignment or when faced with challenges. I am persistent. I am courageous. I am strong. I am energetic! I could list a host of other synonyms, so what I want you to know is this: I am RESILIENT!

Resilience: The Ingredients of a Firm Foundation is my life story, or lifes' story of the growing pains that come with living with two parents who suffered with chronic illness and disabilities. I was a victim of sexual abuse and unhealthy relationships, yet self-discovery and discipline through salvation helped me to find the strength to overcome it *all* in a way that glorifies God. Accepting God's will for my life took hard work, and I had to learn to exchange the lies I believed about myself and begin to see myself as God saw me. I was not a failure, nor was I a mistake. I was a child of God and He said that I was more than a conquer. Baby, I have arrived!

It's my prayer and hope that when you've finished *Resilience: The Ingredients of a Firm Foundation* that you too will find your purpose in this life. Hard work, forgiveness, empathy, and faith are the tools you will need, and believe it or not, you already have what it takes to achieve your greatest level of potential. For you have been created in the very image of God and He declares that you have the ability to do even greater works than He who created you.

Before God formed me in my mother's womb, He was intentional about my purpose. In fact, He strategically mapped out the course of my life; every aspect of it is a part of my destiny. Every trial and all of the tribulations are a part of His plan according to the Word of God. I certainly didn't know it as a child. In fact, I often questioned God on why He would allow me to experience the many things that left me feeling like He didn't love or care for me.

Romans 8:28 says that all things work together for the good of those who are called according to His purpose. Each obstacle, despite its intention to destroy me, has a purpose within itself; they have become the foundation for my life. And my resilience to each one provided me with the courage and the strength to stand whilst making room for spiritual growth.

The first time I heard the story of Joseph, I was moved by our similar connection. Don't get me wrong: my daddy didn't buy me no coat nor did my brothers put me in a pit, but it was the parts of Joseph's life in which he struggled to overcome his situations that I most identified with. Unlike Joseph, I would get angry when I heard lies about myself from others. My blood would boil because the hearer believed it and would hold it against me even while knowing my heart. My dear friend, Mrs. Robinson, would tell me time and time again to stop defending the lies, and that I would outlive them every time. It didn't make sense then, but I have lived long enough to see how the truth ultimately comes to light. What was meant to harm Joseph, God used to define his purpose as well as bless his family, including those same brothers who left him for dead in that pit. What's important here is the coat favored and covered Joseph, and it was the reason his brothers hated him.

Joseph had been rejected by his brothers, sold into slavery, left for dead and imprisoned. He'd avoided sexual advances from his boss, Pharaoh's wife, while also being lied upon. Yet none of the obstacles he endured were able to block his blessing or prevent God's plan from coming to fruition. God's plan, for those unfamiliar with the story, was to develop Joseph's character for the God-ordained purpose and assignment of providing food for the nation during a famine, and Joseph did just that. God would never take us to a place where we were unequipped to perform His work.

Joseph's brother's actions ultimately put him in a position to reign over them. Unlike most of us, Joseph did not use his power to impose sanctions on his family, because let's be clear: he could have. Instead, Joseph opted to show grace, the same grace God was able to show me. In the end, Joseph and his family reunited. And, Joseph lived his life understanding who God was to him—and he to God. Within the pages of *Resilience: The Ingredients of a Firm Foundation* are intimate parts of my life's story, that with therapy and faith in God have made me less vulnerable, while also providing the truth on which I stand: God has loved me from my very beginning. It is my hope that while reading *Resilience: The Ingredients of a Firm Foundation* you not only see how God mapped out my life with intention and purpose, but that He can do the same for you. I am thankful for my family and appreciate their loving me the best they could. And despite what the enemy may have designed for evil in my life, God—being true to His word—turned it for good.

Enjoy the read.

1

"Before I formed you in the womb I knew you, before you were born I set you apart; I appointed you as a prophet to the nations." Jerimiah 1:5

IT WAS 1967 when Lillian Leola Stuart, my mother, was five months pregnant with me when her right leg was amputated due to bone cancer. According to stories shared, my mother complained for months before a doctor took her seriously and ordered a biopsy. Leola was certainly known to be a real drama queen when she was in pain. She would scream bloody murder over a finger pinch and if you happened to be in earshot it was likely that you also thought she was being murdered, given the degrees of pain expressed. However, I'm pretty sure this pain was different; somehow, it silenced her screams while building resilience through her discomfort. Lillian Leola Stuart was no medical professional, but like most women, she knew her body.

My mother was 37 years old and five months pregnant with her fifth child when she learned she had bone cancer and would become an amputee. I can only imagine how helpless and afraid she must have felt learning that there was a possibility that she could lose me before giving birth. I wonder if she even understood what that diagnosis meant? Did she think it would be a pill she could take to cure the cancer? Or did she think that the diagnosis was an automatic death sentence? I regret not having asked her more questions about this time in her life.

During this time, both my mother and my father, John Matthew Stuart, were estranged from their families, which helped neither, as each could have benefited from the support of a family member. My father worked as a heavy equipment operator. He drove those big construction trucks during the week and on the weekends, he worked at a news stand. Fortunately for them they had a small nucleus of friends that were supportive and proved to be most valuable to our family.

The stress of learning one has cancer can be daunting. I'm certain the "What if's" of undergoing major surgery while pregnant was sure to be difficult to handle to say the least, as the stress alone proposed great risk to her unborn baby. Between 0 and 37 weeks the chances of having a premature baby increase at the level of stress the mother may encounter. Some studies suggest that stress in the womb can affect a baby's temperament and neurobehavioral development. Additionally, infants whose mothers experienced high levels of stress while pregnant, particularly in the first trimester, show signs of more depression and irritability.

TIP People who are supported by close relationships with friends, family, or fellow members of a church are less vulnerable to ill health and premature death. The benefits to one's mental health when having a good support system are reported as having a higher survival rate than those who don't. Studies have also shown that social support can reduce depression and anxiety. A strong support system can often reduce stress.

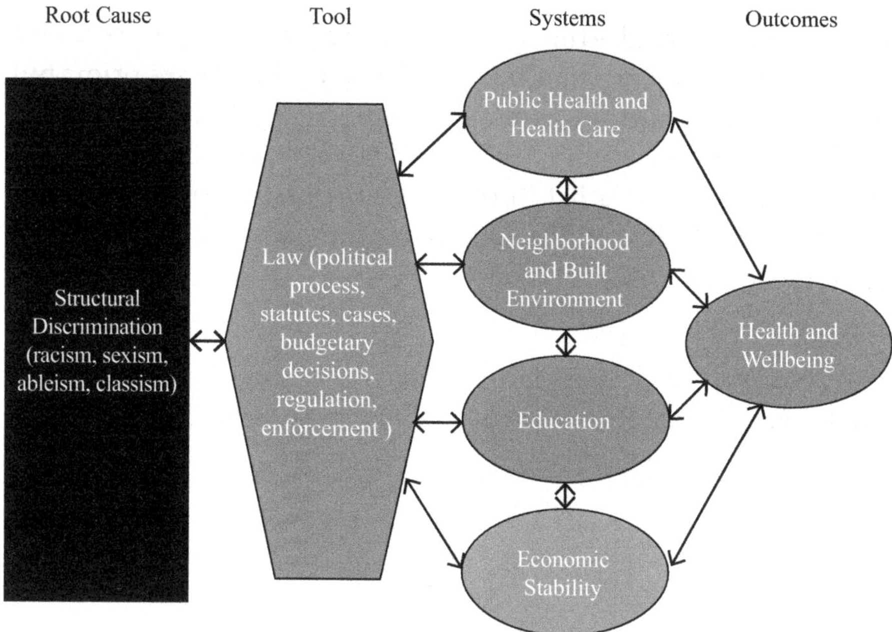

Revised SDOH Framework created by Ruqaiijah Yearby (2020)

Treatment for bone cancer in the late 1960s depended on the type, how far it had spread, and the general health of the person. Furthermore, the first chemotherapy drug discovered to be effective in reducing tumors in patients who had no satisfactory result from radiation wasn't approved by the Food and Drug Administration until 1962, which could explain the limited experience of my mother's physicians. Additionally, I would be remiss to not mention how there was very little trust between African Americans and the medical profession. Ironically enough Dr. Gardner remained our primary physician up until I married. There's something to be said about loyalty. I always question why patients remain with the same doctor even though they aren't happy with their level of care. Despite Dr. Gardner's poor start, he did manage to be of great help and was able to address the concerns everyone had around the risk to the unborn baby, the risk to my mother's life, as well as the quality of life after if—God forbid—the worst was to occur. Fortunately for us, a chemotherapy drug had been approved a few years prior, but it was still new, and the effects on unborn children hadn't been confirmed. Either way in 1967; a 37-year-old African American female did not have a list of options to consider for a treatment plan that would lead to her surviving the cancer and not losing her unborn child.

TIP Structural Racism: Laws which discriminated against African Americans and enforced racial segregation between Whites and Blacks. These laws ended in 1965.

Because my mother's pain was located below her knee, the doctors were unable to determine if the cancer had spread above it, and the risk of a second surgery if all the cancer wasn't removed the first time could prove to be too much for her; the same risk applied to chemotherapy. Her only option in removing the cancer, as she reminded me daily, was to remove the entire leg because she was pregnant with me, another fact she never let me forget. If she had not been pregnant she could have withstood a limb salvage surgery, or even the possibility of two surgeries that would have saved her leg. Losing her leg to bone cancer changed her entire life, yet it did not define her. My mother was a strong woman, resilient and well abled, and we both survived.

2

On the day you were born the angels got together and decided to create a dream come true...

TUESDAY, JULY 18TH, 1967, five months after having her leg removed, my mother and Aunt Helen, were riding in the back of an ambulance where she would finally meet me. Aunt Helen was the person you just loved to be around. She lived relatively close to my mother with her husband MC. When they brought me home from the hospital Uncle MC called me Olive Oyl after *Popeye's* girlfriend. I guess to him we were about the same size; ain't nobody called me that since since–just in case you were wondering.

Aunt Helen's smile made me feel loved and wanted. She was a true lady and carried herself as such; she attended church regularly and sang in the choir. I felt welcomed every time I visited. Going to her home was like going to Grandma's house. In the family room were cabinets filled with knick-knacks she'd collected over the years. Her furniture was covered in the kind of plastic you never wanted to get stuck sitting on in the summer with shorts on. The curtains that hung were white with tiny flowers printed on them. I spent many weekends with my siblings and cousins sitting on the floor "making too much noise" as we played and watched the television while our parents sat around the table in the next room laughing and talking. Aunt Helen could tell a story just with her facial expressions. Her eyes became really big when she told the story of how my mother had become frantic when she'd learned her water had broken. Aunt Helen said she screamed a lot, and I believe her account of that evening's events only because my mother was known to be a drama queen. From what I understand, Mrs. Leola shouted every curse word that came to mind, so much so that the medical attendants along with Aunt Helen thought it was the phantom pain she often cried about since having her leg amputated. Folks kept trying to reassure her that she was fine, but she wasn't. I'm certain the dismissal of my mother's pain that day was reminiscent of years passed; and what came next was nothing to blink at.

"It's not my *fucking* leg. It's my *mother fucking* finger," my mother boldly stated, leaving everyone embarrassed and maybe a little offended. She had a way of saying something that landed as hard as she intended it. Apparently in a rush to get my mother to the hospital, her finger had been smashed between the bed rail on the gurney and because it was covered up with the sheets no one noticed.

Understanding how dramatic my mom could be, reminds me of another story a nurse shared with me when my mother was in the nursing home right before she passed away. She was so different in her latter years. In her last two years she was more kindhearted, and she curbed her abusive language. I never heard her curse at me or anyone, which made caring for her the last two years of her life easy. If she became upset it caused conflict for me emotionally. I had always told myself I could never move my mom into my home to care for her, believing it would be too much for me. It was important to be able to provide care without being resentful. Nevertheless, I was able to have her transferred to a facility about 15 minutes from my home in NJ, and about 20 minutes from where she lived in Pennsylvania. God knew.

While in the nursing home, my mom had a roommate. They'd been together about three weeks or so. I was usually her only visitor during the day, and once a month a faithful Deacon Johnson would come to give my mom communion. My mom didn't talk to the lady and she didn't complain or fuss about much else at this point. I guess she had gone through enough medically that she was more at peace than I ever remember. She had a cell phone and some spare change in her drawer—nothing major, just enough to get a Pepsi from the vending machine. I also brought her a Pepsi every day when I visited. When I got off work, I would stop at a store or restaurant and get something I knew she loved, like crab cakes, or shrimp to take for her dinner.

On this one day the roommate, thinking my mother was cognitively unaware of her presence went rummaging through my mother's drawer. My mother might have been sleeping or just had her eyes closed, and you know the saying about every shut eye ain't always sleep. Amy, my mother's nurse, happened to be walking past the room as my mother was fussing at the roommate, "*Get your black ass out of my shit, you know damn well that ain't yours. You ol'bitch always in somebody shit!*" Amy said she ran in the room to see the lady walking back over to her bed, and my mother saying "*Get your black ass out of here!*" as the lady walked away. I knew not one word was a lie as I listened to Amy retell that story. I laughed so hard because my mother was still that fiery little tongue lasher I remembered, and despite her perceived vulnerability, she was never completely defenseless.

My father randomly said "*Charlene looks just like Charlie,*" to my mother after she had given birth to me; this was the story my parents told me when explaining how I got my name. There was no discussion of my name prior to my birth, so it was a shock to my mom. My dad named me after my big brother, Charles David Stuart.

My mother, Mrs. Leola, had five children she gave birth to and one she legally adopted. I have five brothers and three sisters. Charlie and I had the same mother and father. My three older siblings were Lorraine (aka Sister), George (aka Cal) and Kevin (aka Bubba). When Lorraine was young she couldn't say "Kevin" and called him Bubba, which sounded like brother. Likewise, he could not say her name, so he referred to her as "sister". They were from my mother's first marriage. My father had five other children with his first wife: John Jr., Ruth, George, Blanch (aka Candi), and Joseph (aka Joey). And, now that we are all adults; he likes to be called Joe). My parents adopted my younger brother, Marvin, who came to live with us when he was 18 months old. His mother was unable to care for him, and asked my parents for support. He was legally adopted before he entered middle school.

3

My Story: Perception or Reality

THE FIRST 18 months of my life was spent in the foster care of Dr. Gardner, our White family doctor. It's never been confirmed or even spoken of at any great lengths, but what I do know for certain is that reaching for White women in public was a common practice during my toddler years. If that's not confirmation I don't know what is.

Paternal bonding occurs early and happens when a newborn's skin is touched, during feeding and over basic care. My mother and I weren't able to bond because she was unable to provide care due to the amputation, which could explain why our relationship was as it was.

TIP The evidence from an abundance of research on this subject is very clear. Children who are separated from their parents at birth can have long-lasting traumatic repercussions. Attachment is not just a feeling, it's paramount to the child's development across the lifespan. The bond between a mother and child is first formed in the womb.

I wonder if that scream my mother made when she was on the way to the hospital the night I was born didn't help to shape my hearing, and is perhaps the reason for my dislike of crying of any sort. Despite what the research says, I know I would have rather not been in her presence as a child than be with her, because she was so verbally abusive. I had peace when I knew she was going to be absent for a set length of time or on a bus trip to Atlantic City.

I have no recollection of the time I lived with Dr. Gardner. From what I understand, my brother, Kevin, begged my mom to bring me home, promising to take good care of me. He tried as best he could. The story shared about my return is that after 18 months with the Gardeners; I returned to my mother extremely skinny, I didn't like milk, and my pinky finger was bandaged. I'd gotten stitches as a result of it almost being severed in a car door. To hear my mom tell it, I came home looking like a refugee.

Kevin was very protective of Charlie and me. He was also our hero on more than one occasion. Charlie has more memories of Kevin than I do, but it was Kevin's heroic thinking that saved me and Charlie from the house fire. I wish I could remember Kevin, the brother who handed me and Charlie out the window to awaiting neighbors. I was two years old and Charlie was four. Kevin was 14 when he drowned in a small creek not far from our home. He and Charlie were over at the local YMCA where he worked with other youths playing basketball. Charlie said that Kevin had told the other kids to clean up and to put the athletic equipment away as it was time for the center to close. One of the boys playing with them that day for some reason had kicked the ball into the creek. Kevin had jumped in to get the ball, but not before giving his sneakers and shirt to Charlie, who had held them alongside the bank. Charlie said, *"I watched him swim after the ball, and then I couldn't see him anymore. He was there and then I didn't see him. He was gone."* It was never clear how long Charlie waited before he ran home to my mom to tell her what happened. He was only five years old when Kevin died. I can't imagine what his little self must have thought—the wonder, the fear, the "what ifs" that may have filled his curiosity. Charlie has told me that he still thinks about that day like it just happened. There was no trauma-informed approach in 1970, and there was no crisis intervention that came to talk and help him process watching his older brother drown.

There are two very distinct things that forever connect me to Kevin; one is the burn scar on my right elbow. He'd placed me on the counter too close to the stove while fixing lunch for us. I leaned over and got burned. Kevin was devastated. The other is our sense of humor.

I wish I had known Kevin personally. I have often heard he was always clowning around and being silly, something I definitely inherited. Kevin also shares the same birthday as my granddaughter, who ironically enough nearly drowned.

Rest in Paradise Kevin Greene, November 26, 1956–June 19, 1970.

TIP Separation anxiety and bonding: The significance to the development of a child.

Early maternal separation can result in a series of traumatic emotional reactions, during which the child engages in an anxious period of calling and active search behavior followed by a period of declining behavioral responsiveness.

The bond of mother and child, and learning during this time is very important to the development of the newborn. Research suggests that when a child is separated from the biological mother at birth, it can lead to a list of emotional reactions in the child. A child may engage in anxious behavior, not only in the first few years but throughout his/her lifespan.[1]

Uncle Sammy, who wasn't a blood relative, but the brother of Aunt Jean, one of my mother's best friends, lived in our finished basement with our German Shepherd, Bozo. Uncle Sammy didn't work anywhere formally; he received Social Security. He suffered from alcohol addiction and maybe other mental health issues that went undiagnosed. The unfortunate reality is that most African American families had an Uncle Sammy in their guest room, as support for mental health was non-existent, which left many judged and ostracized. Once every few weeks my mom would make him come upstairs and take a bath and change his clothes. On those days, Uncle Sammy was sure to hit the streets. When he returned he would bring treats back for me—candy or some little trinket he had picked up during his day's travels.

When the ice cream truck came around, Uncle Sammy would give me more than enough money for my Bomb Pop, making it easy to not to ask my mother for ice cream money, because I'd kept Uncle Sammy's change. Uncle Sammy was also the live-in babysitter. My mother would inadvertently assign him the task of sitter when she dipped on us to run errands. Prior to leaving, he would tell Mrs. Leola *"That gal is gonna be lookin' for you like someone kidnapped cha,"* and sure enough as if cued, I would run into the house after coming home from school, screaming at the top of my lungs, *"Mom, Mom!"* My voice would echo through the house. A startled Uncle Sammy would slowly make his way up the basement stairs to dispel the image of abduction that each call for my mom held. He'd find me in the dining room at the table. *"Your mother is at the market,"* Uncle Sammy would say. His voice and presence were reassuring.

Waiting for my mother to return from her errands was like waiting for a time bomb to explode. It didn't matter if I had done my chores, or if my brothers hadn't done theirs; it didn't matter who made the mess or who cleaned it up; I was always the one who received the verbal lashing and sometimes physical punishment, as there was always a reason for her to be upset with me.

By the time I got to middle school I had my mother's errand run clocked down to the minute. Most times she was only gone for no more than two hours, or long enough to spend her monthly check on the house necessities. She would make her shopping rounds at her favorite stores like Roy Tweedy's Fresh Meat Market and Acme. When she was shopping she was in a different space; sometimes she was pleasant. She was even more pleasant when my sister came to visit. She smoked marijuana and shared it with my mom. Those weekends were the best!

Despite the angst in my *"Mom"* calls I almost always wished she wasn't home even when she was. There was never a true longing for her, which was due to our separation at birth, I more so needed to know where she was, so that I knew where to be. Sometimes she would find me, her berating insults not far behind. We struggled to manufacture the bond of mother and child, as life's obstacles imposed upon what would have been time for us. Instead, my mother spent those early years struggling to find herself amidst cancer, being an amputee, a house fire, a flood, the responsibility of being a new mother and the death of Kevin. The underlying effects of both compound and complex trauma certainly influenced her parenting—or the lack thereof.

I wasn't the only one who resented Mrs. Leola's choice words; Uncle Sammy struggled with her proclivity to profanity and demeaning others, so much so that he would sob whenever my mother began one of her tirades. His sobs seemed to come from a place of helplessness, combined with a sense of guilt for possibly being unable to protect me from her. He often would say he wished he could take me away, but that wasn't possible because he wasn't able. Uncle Sammy favored me over my two brothers;

however, as I got older and began to develop into a young woman, Uncle Sammy changed some, especially when he was drinking. It's rare that people understand the weight of their words. In the Bible it speaks of the tongue holding life or death. Sometimes Uncle Sammy's tongue was deadly.

TIP Complex post-traumatic stress disorder is closely related to traditional post-traumatic stress disorder (PTSD). PTSD is a psychiatric disorder that can develop after a person experiences a traumatic event. Complex PTSD, also known as CPTSD, can result if a person experiences prolonged or repeated trauma over months or years. A person with the condition may experience additional symptoms to those that define PTSD.[2]

The old childhood saying *"Sticks and stones may break my bones, but names will never hurt me"* is a lie! Words have power; they have the ability to cause lifelong damage. My mother's words, worse only to those of a drunken sailor in a bar room fight, would often cut to my core and kill my entire soul, which often left me feeling less than a human and unworthy of love.

TIP: Verbal aggression alone turns out to be a particularly strong risk factor for depression, anger-hostility, and dissociative disorders. The latter involve cutting off a particular mental function from the rest of the mind. In one type of dissociation, the person can't recall part of his or her personal history.[3]

4

"Life isn't how to survive the storm, it's about how to dance in the rain "~ Taylor Swift

MY MOTHER WAS a country girl. She was one of seven children born and raised in Church Road, just outside of Petersburg, Virginia, where farmland and woods lived for miles. The houses were miles apart from one another, separated only by long dark winding roads. There were no sidewalks or street lights, which helped make the night darker. Most times you couldn't see your hand in front of your face, yet in the midst of nature was the darkness that trailed from those country roads with Mrs. Leola right on up the interstate to New York City.

My mother's first marriage was to George Cutter Greene, but we called him Wert. Their marriage was both toxic and dysfunctional. Wert was an alcoholic, and according to my family, he and my mother fought regularly. My Aunts, Nancy and Ida, and my cousin, Peter, who lived in New York, made frequent trips to Hackensack where they'd moved to. Like many African Americans, the pair moved from the rural south of Virginia to the North in search of better employment opportunities while escaping the laws of the Jim Crow south.

TIP Historical trauma is cumulative emotional and psychological pain experienced by a mass of people over a lifespan or across generations.

Despite the couple's volatile relationship, they brought three children into their otherwise-unstable home. The impact of being in the midst of such conflict would show itself later.

TIP Effects of domestic violence on children. Children who witness violence between parents may also be at a higher risk of being violent in their future relationships. Children may blame themselves for the abuse; they may have low self-esteem, or may be withdrawn in social settings such as school during gym. More than 15 million children in the United States live in homes in which domestic violence has happened at least once.[4]

Around 1963, my mother abandoned her husband and three young children. Why? I don't know. I surmise that the abuse was too much. And the affair she had with my father could have factored into her decision. Mrs. Leola and my biological father—who also abandoned his wife and five children—migrated to Media, Pennsylvania. Once they moved to Pennsylvania, it was like a plague had fallen on them. Though nothing of biblical proportions, yet in a span of three years, they were estranged from their families, lost a home to a fire, her leg was amputated because of bone cancer, one of their children tragically drowned and they lost everything to a flood. All things considered, I am reminded of the story of Job, who lost everything. Instead of receiving support from his friends and family, they saw his misfortune as a sign that God must be punishing him. I'm grateful to know that God is not so cruel. In the Bible, God says the rain falls on the just and the unjust, which means the experience of calamity is fair game, but more importantly God is not doing the punishing. A great man of God once said, "God is not that angry, because He dispensed His anger at the cross."

The internal struggle endured; the fact that no one has ever seen her break speaks volumes to her strength and intrinsic will, which—to some degree—proved to be both a blessing and a curse. I'm certain the PTSD is what made it appear that she also had or could be diagnosed as being someone with Intermittent Explosive Disorder. Unfortunately the disorders combined left us in the care of someone suffering with impulsivities couched in verbal abuse. Yet at the same time she held within her a tenacious fire and stern will not to be vulnerable in a manner that left her defenseless. Her words were her buckler, and her demeanor always acted as her shield which allowed her, in her own way, to dance in the rain juxtaposed living within her storms.

For example, if she was in a public place and needed to use the restroom and the one handicapped stall was occupied, she would intentionally wait for the person to exit before using the restroom. If the occupant wasn't visibly handicapped, she would verbally lash out and make that person know how insensitive it was for them to use the only space for those in wheelchairs when multiple stalls existed for those without, leaving the person full of shame, guilt, and most likely the knowledge that they would never be doing that again!

TIP Emotional Intelligence: the capacity to be aware of, control, and express one's emotions, and to handle interpersonal relationships judiciously and empathetically.
Emotional intelligence is the key to both personal and professional success.

Some of the symptoms you might see in victims with complex trauma could be trust, changes in self-perception, guilt, shame, or helplessness. If my mother suffered with any of these, and I'm sure she probably did, you wouldn't have known by looking at her.

However, clinically she had all the signs and coping skills that suggested she was suffering with mental health issues as a result of the trauma she'd previously endured. Had Mrs. Leola surrendered her will to God, I know He could have used her trauma and made it all work for her good, but she didn't. However, I was in my mid 20s when I learned of God's grace, and how in our weaknesses He makes us strong, which is more than enough to prevent a flex or a crush to anyone's spirit.

This history of complex trauma must have had long-term effects that would become a part of what made her the aggressive, demanding, and demeaning authoritarian I saw growing up. As I would discover, it was my very presence that sometimes triggered the negative exchanges shared between my mother and me. One could say we were doomed from the beginning; perhaps she blamed me for the loss of her entire leg because she was pregnant with me at the time of diagnosis, and was presented with limited options. But those are the conversations that are dismissed and slowly morph into something less containable. For my mother, that meant using her words as weapons because she couldn't speak to anyone, as therapy at that time was unheard of in the Black community, making it easy for her to nurture the dysfunction that had festered unaddressed. It was common to be called ugly names, which made me vulnerable to predators—my mother included.

TIP Emotionally, children develop in the direction of greater self-awareness—i.e., awareness of their own emotional states, characteristics, and potential for action—and they become increasingly able to discern and interpret the emotions of other people. This contributes to empathy, or the ability to appreciate the feelings and perceptions of others and understand their points of view.

5

"She can be attractive, intelligent, and successful and yet feel like she is unworthy of love, or see herself as less than." ~ unknown

ABUSE IS LIKE an ugly cancer that, little by little, eats away at your soul, self-confidence, esteem, and worth. While in an abusive relationship your sense of self fades, leaving you vulnerable, which impedes your judgment as it relates to the abuse[er]. The emotional dichotomy becomes more difficult when the abuser is someone like a close family member, friend, or even a parent, spouse or intimate partner. Women who have been emotionally abused in childhood might posture that behavior while in their relationships by allowing themselves to feel undeserving of love in a healthy way. Often, these women will stay in abusive and toxic relationships, uncertain of what a healthy relationship looks like, and will justify their "situation" as love, in an effort to cover up the abuse. Not all abusers intend to destroy their victims, however, they almost always intend on controlling the victim, which is a spirit of emotional manipulation rooted in witchcraft.

Parents, over everyone else in a child's life, have the greatest opportunity to emotionally destroy a child. I've heard that a girl's mother is the most influential person in her life. From her, she will learn to be either a nurturer or an abuser. In fact, research suggests that if a child's first interactions earlier in development are rooted in abuse, it's almost certain to be a common pattern in future relationships.[5]

I have experienced a few relationships that could have been toxic if I had remained in them. I once dated a man who was single, and, for the first time, *I knew for sure he was single* and I wanted it to be my last relationship. He was always available, which meant I never had to question his dating status or availability. After about three weeks of long conversations and intimate sharing with him, we mutually decided that we were in a relationship, which went public amongst our families and friends. However, it should have ended after the second date. It was during this time that our relationship began to take a turn, and I began to ignore my own boundaries, which gave him license to trespass as well. Trusting him, I'd confided in him about the sexual abuse I'd endured and disclosed how important it was for me to be with a partner who would be consciously considerate with all things and would ensure my comfort in all spaces. He said all the right things, yet despite being open and transparent with him, he too forced me to do something I wasn't ready to do.

We had spent a few days talking on the phone because I knew he was really single and not lying to me, at least in my thirsty head LOL. I thought he must be the one, right? We went out on the Friday, and the first red flag should have been the place he took me. It was a hole-in-the wall dive bar! It was like Cheers, where Norm was a bar stool favorite: everybody knew his name. We spent a few hours sitting and chatting in this dark dingy bar and I was soon over it. Since it wasn't so late he told me about the park where everyone hung out during the summer. For what could have been most of the night we talked in the park and shared stories. I felt safe, respected, and I felt that he heard me. He heard me! The next night we hung out again, but this time the place was an actual restaurant that I had picked. After dinner we went back to the park and sat in the car listening to music and talking until 3am or so when I'd offered to take him home...*to his mother's house.* He said that his mom told him to not let me ride home alone; if we should ever stay out late again, and that I should just stay at her house. I thought *"Oh wow how sweet and considerate of her not having met me but still opening up her home."* Taking them both up on the offer I agreed to stay and we headed back to the house. We were sitting in the living room when he jumped from the chair he'd been sitting in and demanded that I stand up and turn around. There he stood in front of me with his pants down around his legs, holding his penis. Shock and disappointment ran through me like a slow current. His command was familiar, and as if a switch to comply was flipped on inside of me. I subconsciously gave into his coercion; sadly, it was something I had done many times before. My mind wandered to thoughts of worst case scenarios: complying—although the worst—seemed to be the only option that would get me home, which was all I wanted at the moment. It wasn't long before reflection set in and forced the harsh reality that Nate was no better than the others who had pretended to see me long enough to get what they wanted. He threw my fears of being rejected back at me, leaving me to contemplate "what if he gets angry" and the aftermath of dealing with my own resolve, should he decide he didn't want to see me again. My brain processed his command and without protest, I stood up and took my clothes off reminiscent of times past; before him stood ten-year-old Charlene whose hands were forced to touch another penis, another day, by someone who said they cared.

Dating was interesting for me. I was taught through the church that you should abstain from sex and all sexual activity, and that includes oral sex; some folks have that twisted, it's all sex. In addition, one should only engage in sexual activity with a spouse, which basically means abstinence before marriage. I found that once I'd started dating it didn't take long, maybe within the first three dates, that sex was there. So I avoided dating for long periods because I couldn't understand why I wasn't finding men that wanted the same as I did when it came to relationships. I thought something was fundamentally wrong with me, and blamed it on the energy I was putting out, because what else would cause me to attract the exact opposite of what I wanted?

If I was dating and the guy insisted on touching and kissing me, I never stopped him; I simply complied, and it wasn't until someone asked me why I hadn't said no to Nate that I recognized the pattern of not being able to say no. Determined to make changes in my dating life, I began to search for answers that helped me put things together; rooted in my search was 10-year-old Charlene who'd been coerced to touch her abuser's penis after he forced her hands down his pants.

When I was aged 10, Chris, a self-imposed godfather and family friend took my "no" and held it for longer than I care to admit. Growing up, the topic of sex in my home was open and unprohibited, and not nearly as guarded a subject as one would have thought, and because of that I didn't know that engaging in sexual acts was wrong. Chris did what he wanted to me and forced me to do things to him. The only time I can remember him not thinking of himself was at the sound of heavy footsteps. On one occasion he had come over to our house earlier that day and instructed me to meet him in the basement. Our basement had a bed that he would often make use of. Most times in the basement, he would not only touch and fondle me; he would also perform cunnilingus. As an adult, I struggled for a very long time to reconcile how it made me feel juxtaposed the abuse I'd experienced.

One night as we lay on the bed, he tried to penetrate me with his penis after performing oral sex. It hurt so badly that I started to cry. He didn't press me to continue; instead, he kissed me, assuring me that everything would be okay with practice. I didn't mind doing what he told me because when he touched me, it didn't hurt, and the dichotomy for me was that I enjoyed his kisses and his hands on my vagina. It felt good, and my body responded naturally, which I had no control over. Chris was a crafty predator, as most are; he groomed me into believing that I needed to practice, and he was willing to teach me. Not having a true reference for love and how it should look and feel made it easy for him to groom me, and as time would have it, Chris would soon be the image of "boyfriend" that I'd created even well after he'd moved away and married. I believed he loved me.

Fighting through guilt and shame to accept that Chris was wrong and that I wasn't emotionally defective, it was necessary to go back to the beginning, when as a kid I had learned about sex through the pornography rooted in our home. It was nothing for me to walk into my living room and see sex on television. My siblings and I were never asked to leave a room, nor was there a warning to not enter; sex was on television like the evening news. My mother never fussed about my father's movies nor about us kids watching the adults watch adults, because she knew our father would never hurt us. And he didn't, at least not physically.

My failure to stand firmly on not wanting to proceed any further with Nate left me with great disappointment. I wished I had spoken up for myself and said *No, I don't want to do this!* We had spent hours and days talking about failed relationships and how this time I really wanted something different. He seemed to understand that I wanted a relationship that wasn't all about the sex, and that was grounded in a true friendship. He knew I wanted respect and was looking for someone to love me for me. But I didn't say no. I don't think I knew how to say no and really mean it. It was later as I began to grow and understand relationships that I realized what I always wanted was intimacy; I just wasn't able to communicate that and wouldn't have recognized it even if it were standing in my face. For many years I thought intimacy was sexual behavior, because of a distorted perception of sex and love. There is a shame and remorse that I feel from time to time for complying, but there is no condemnation to those who are in Christ Jesus.

The impact on my cognitive development and understanding of sex was devastating. When thinking about intellectual or cognitive development, one should think beyond learning the academic skills of building knowledge. Cognitive and intellectual development are much broader than just learning colors, shapes, and letters of the alphabet. In fact, they are really centered on how the brain changes as we learn and grow. Children process events based on their understanding and experiences. Jean Piaget, a Swiss psychologist who developed theories of cognitive development after observing children through experiments said that children whose experience matches what they understand are in a state of equilibrium. I didn't understand how what I saw in pornography stimulated me, but I knew it had an effect on me. In an effort to satisfy the desires I felt, I would straddle something hard, rub and grind my vagina over and over the arm of the sofa or on my brother's baseball bats, sometimes making myself sore. Yet almost daily I would try to satisfy the need that tingled in my body. By the time Chris began touching me, I liked it more than I did when I tried to satisfy myself. He didn't hurt me as I hurt myself when I manipulated myself on the hard objects. He felt good. I loved it, and like an addict chasing their first high, I spent most of my adult life chasing that erotic feeling of pleasure that I'd received in an unconventional way of masturbation and the oral stimulation I received from Chris.

My journey to overcoming my negative past hasn't been easy. I was good at pleasing people and had a distorted perception of helping versus pleasing for approval. Being a people pleaser was a skill I learned as a little girl. I felt that if I could do everything my mother expected, and even those things not mentioned, it would cause her to fuss at me less, and she would love and accept me more. No matter how hard I tried, there was always something that would set the silence into a raging fire with the hurtful words she used. I would sit in stillness for hours in our family room as I waited for the sound of her waking up. The silence was peaceful and calm, yet it held so much fear. I was as fearful of the storm that could come the moment she woke up. When she woke up, through her closed door I heard her voice coming from her room, my name being called, CHARLENE. Not waiting for the next word, I always responded YES, HERE I COME!

Contemplating how I could escape the grips of my mother some nights was consuming. Often, I thought of ways to end her life, something I wrestled with for years. In those moments I would dream vividly of chasing her to bring about harm or even kill her. It was the same vivid dream for years; I chased her down a dark street after finally being freed—from what or where was never a vision in the dream, but I would be running down this dark street, knife in hand, ready to stab my mother over and over again, only my mother was not visible in the dream, just her wheelchair. I was in my late 30s the last time I had that dream.

Realizing that although the feelings I had toward my mother were not "normal" as much as they were real, I thought it necessary to speak with someone. One day I went to speak to my former pastor about the relationship between me and my mother. I did not tell him the worst of what she could be, for example when she would curse me out simply for not calling her by a certain time, or how I was failing at parenting my son—something she reminded me of constantly. I shared just enough information to prompt this reply from him. "You don't have to live with that type of mental abuse." He stated without so much as a scripture; in fact he said what I wanted to hear, which was that I had every right to walk off and never speak to my mother again.

Healing takes time; however, healing with God is a process. I started the process shortly after getting saved. In Christ I learned to see myself as God saw me, which was no easy task, especially since, over the years, belief of what others said and thought of me had already taken root. God reminds us to let the mind of Christ be within us. I had to renew my thinking, and that meant exchanging the lies for the truth. I am not a failure; I am in fact more than a conqueror; I am the apple of His eye; He calls me and you friend! It took a lot of self-talk, reminding myself through positive affirmation that I was the head and not the tail, whilst confirming that as long as I put my faith and trust in Him that I could do all things.

Forgiveness was powerful in helping me to understand how all things worked together for my good, just as God said it would. I've learned how to see the good even in the worst of things. Although I honored both of my parents by respecting them, while never once speaking back, within my heart lived anger and resentment for my mother. There was no way I could receive God's blessing with unresolved anger in my heart. The worst part was that everything I hated about her, I could see reflected in myself as a parent. I hated that I yelled and verbally assaulted my son when he'd done something wrong. Some years prior I'd heard a preacher say how, as individuals, we have both the good and bad of our parents within us. And it's up to us to determine the characteristics we want to keep and the ones to discard. Having decided early that I didn't want my son to feel about me the way I often felt about my mother, I committed to being mindful of my mother's example of parenting, being careful not to present her to him. Instead of using my words to crush his spirit, I opted to build him up by reminding him of the greatness within and that he was able to do anything he put his hands to!

Asking God to teach me how to forgive my mother meant being open to seeing her differently. My mother had her issues, and I had mine. Though that pastor told me I had the right to disown her, I *knew* that wasn't what the word of God taught me. I needed a second opinion. About three years later, while standing in the office of Bishop, another pastor, I shared with him a situation that had arisen between my mother and me, and how I was torn over getting her a birthday gift. Every time I said "but" he would reply "What does the bible say?" We went back and forth in that office for about 30 minutes. He never budged and I knew he was right. I just needed my heart and head to align. This was my first lesson in forgiveness. I embraced the weight of trauma and dysfunctional parenting techniques; I allowed God to work on my heart, so that I could move past the abuse to fully see how God would work it together for my good. Once I trusted God with my concerns regarding my mother and committed to a change of mindset, things began to look and feel immediately differently. Prior to the second pastoral advice of honoring your mother and father that your days be long, I'd been traveling back and forth to Philadelphia after moving to New Jersey to attend Missionary Training School. I had to take public transportation everywhere because I had no car, which forced me to leave the house every Monday and Tuesday around 2pm to make all my connections to get to class on time. Michael, my one and only son, was a latch-key kid. He would come home from school on those days to dinner waiting in the microwave and instructions on what time he was to finish his homework, eat dinner, and wrap up watching television. At the time I didn't have a cell phone so I had to use the pay phone at the school to call him every night at around 6pm. The first night he answered and all was well.

Usually my mother, who was good at controlling others with fear of the unknown, would call Mikey when he arrived home, reminding him to lock the doors, and not to answer to anyone. By the time I got to school, and was able to call and check on him, the phone would ring and ring because he would be asleep. The anxiety of leaving him to go to Philadelphia before he got home was real: What if something happened? Who would he call if he needed help?

The night prior to speaking with Bishop about forgiveness, I had been calling Mikey for hours with no answer. Frantic, I called Bishop and asked if he could send someone over to check on him. Up until that night, I never knew my mother was calling him and putting the fear of God in him. Somehow, she'd managed to convince him to move the furniture to barricade himself in. He did so, then went to sleep shortly thereafter, leaving me to die from worry. In the midst of my worry, God told me that Mike was waterproofed and that everything that belonged to me was covered by God Himself. Scripture instructs believers to train up a child in the way they should go. As long as I did my part, I was reassured that God would cover and protect my seed. He did so then, and continues to keep him covered with favor and grace today.

But the blessing to the obedience was when my mother called that Wednesday night to say that she and my stepfather would be taking me to buy a new car the next day! Talk about a right-now type of God! I earnestly wanted to do what was right; I sought out good counsel, and after making up my mind to forgive, it was immediately rewarded.

6

Trauma informed care: "not asking what have you done, but instead asking what's happened to you?"

IT WAS DURING my mid-forties that my mother became Mrs. Leola whenever I would address her. Our relationship was unique and a far stretch from the "mother-daughter bond" expectation of most women. I loved my mother and I knew my mother loved me, yet there was definitely something different about her parenting.

There are four main styles of parenting: permissive, authoritative, neglectful, and authoritarian. Growing up, I was not neglected, nor was I raised in a home where the child dictated the rules. Mrs. Leola was not having that! If life was a fairytale, then maybe it would have been an authoritative home where problems were solved over meaningful conversations and interactions—you know, like the Brady Bunch. Unfortunately, my mother was not Carol, and she made it clear that it was either her way or the highway. My dad's temper was just as hot and fierce as hers. Once, he slapped my mother so hard I thought her head was going to fall off! They had been fussing about something and my mother continued to berate him. As he attempted to walk away from her, she blocked him and then—POW! He'd open handedly slapped her right upside her head. Shocked, I watched in disbelief, but I was glad for him. I hated how she would badger both my biological father and my stepfather when she argued with them. Mrs. Leola shut up after he slapped her, but revenge was brewing. As my father turned to walk out the house, she threw her Pepsi at his head. Fortunately for him, the door was closing behind him, and the Pepsi bottle hit the back of the door, leaving shattered glass and Pepsi residue. Sometimes my dad lived in our house, and other times he lived across the street in an apartment over top of a bar. Despite their tumultuous relationship there was love and loyalty between them. My mother would always say that she would never turn her back on my father because of the way he cared for her during her recovery after the amputation. While my father was in the hospital, and for many years even up to his death, she made sure he wanted for nothing.

My step-father, Mr. Leroy, AKA "Jar Head" was the complete opposite of my father. He was soft spoken, never speaking above a whisper and never angry. Well actually once he came home from work so upset with his boss and kept telling my brothers and me that he was going to buy his boss a Mother's Day card. We were confused because we knew his boss was a man. Why would you send him a Mother's Day card? we asked. His reply was because he's a BITCH! That's the kind of man he was, calm, cool, and collected.

The Jar Head was a retired vet who had served in the Marines during the Korean War, where he sustained an injury that ended his military career. When he and my mother argued, I always wished he would just once speak up and defend himself, or serve my mother with one of those open hand slaps from time to time. But he never did, not even when she would grip him by the collar; he always remained composed. He allowed nothing to knock him off his square.

The relationship between both my fathers was amazing. My biological father, John [Johnny] dubbed me his "boy" and my stepfather,

Mr. Leroy made me feel like I was special, and he also favored me over my two brothers. He also helped me with my chores, so I wouldn't get in trouble with my mother. When I was in my first semester of college at Cheyney University, he would drive me back after my weekend visits. A Cheney alum; he was excited that I was attending his alma mater. On the way back he would take me to my favorite sandwich store so I could get my famous Tiny Tee's Dollar Hoagie. Once Mr. Leroy found out I was pregnant, it tickled him to think that our stop at Tiny Tee's was somehow for my baby. He would get such a kick out of his own funnies. Mr. Leroy would give me anything I asked for, do anything to support whatever I was doing in school, and when I was looking for a job, he put in a good word for me at State Liquor Store, where he was an assistant manager. I still had to go through the interview process, but I got the job working beside him. I worked there for almost a year before I had the baby. He was also the one who taught me about dating. He often coached me on never letting a man break me to the point of crying, and to make sure I understood my self-worth. It took several years of failed relationships before getting that lesson.

I don't remember when he moved in with us exactly, but I remember him living with us prior to 1976, the year my niece was born. Before that, my mother would fix his dinner and take it to his job. I would ride with her. My mother would drive and park the car behind the liquor store and wait for him to come out. Mr. Leroy would walk out to the car and stand outside the driver's window. They would chat for a few seconds before she handed him the food. He never spoke directly to me, but he spoke about me to my mother. Once close enough to the car where he could see me, he would always ask my mother *why I looked so mean.* On the way back home, my mother would press me on whether I liked him. What was I gonna tell her? No, I don't like him? I didn't know that man from a can of paint. I didn't respond, but I did wonder if my dad knew about him. It wasn't long before he was living with us too!

On the way home from dropping off Mr. Leroy's plate; Mrs. Leola would drive past the bar where my dad worked to drop off his food. She would park the car and head into the house; I would run across the lot super excited to bring him his dinner. Most times when I walked in he would say *"Here comes my boy."* One time I had a scarf on my head and he flipped out, which also happened to be the only time he yelled at me. When I entered he screamed, *"What the hell is that on your head? Take that shit off looking like Aunt Jamama. And don't you ever come out of the house looking that ever again!"*

I don't ever recall my parents fussing with one another, nor do I recall hearing either of them fuss about the other. We were a family by definition and actions. On some occasions the three of them lived together and other times my father lived across the street, but he would still come by and more so for overnight visits. Funny, I never saw my family as different, despite the obvious dysfunction. It was years later when I realized that the three of them were raising us. I was well into my forties when one of my childhood friends made mention over conversation that *everyone knew my three parents were swingers!* You could have knocked me over with a feather when I heard those words: like, really? How did they know and I didn't? The logistics of my parents' unconventional relationships weren't the business of us kids. What was important was that we were cared for and loved.

My biological father passed away in 1996 from renal failure. He was 73 and left behind Mrs. Leola, me and my siblings and Mr. Leroy. My mother attended the funeral, and sat on the front row with me and all my siblings, which caused quite a bit of confusion amongst his family.

7

UNCLE ROBERT, MY mom's brother who lived in Cleveland, Ohio died. It was left to me to get both my mother and Mr. Leroy to the funeral. The price of airline tickets from Philadelphia to Cleveland was well over $700 each and I had to purchase three. I decided to save on the price of tickets by driving to Maryland, and then flying to Ohio from there. I knew the trip was going to be a challenge, especially since my arm was in a soft cast due to a previous injury, nevertheless I borrowed a friend's truck and the three of set off.

We arrived at the airport; after seeking out a female staff member I dropped them off. She'd agreed to take them to the check in desk while I parked. I carefully explained to the attendant that they both needed assistance and requested wheelchairs. Before leaving to park the truck I tipped the attendant $30 and we agreed that we would meet at the gate.

After parking, I hopped on the shuttle and headed back to the airport only to see my parents sitting in the same spot I'd left them, with the attendant nowhere to be found. Frustration began to set in; my arm ached and I knew I wasn't mentally prepared. Still needing to get them to the gate, I came up with what seemed to be a perfect plan. I knew what I was facing was going to be *one to remember,* and certainly not the kind of memory that would bring joy. Yet, as I share this story, I've smiled a lot whilst giving God praise for the grace He's extended to me since.

Both of my parents sat in those wheelchairs looking like two lost children waiting for someone to claim them from lost and found. I walked in and there they sat off to my right. I spotted the restrooms straight ahead and to the left. Quickly I turned and marched toward my escape ignoring them and lamenting all the way in my head. *Why GOD? Why are you punishing me? I prayed this morning, I haven't gotten smart with anyone today. While rushing here to make this flight, I didn't flip the bird: Why, God? Why are they just sitting there? God, I'm a good daughter. I paid $1500 bucks GOD for three plane tickets, God why are they sitting there? God, you see them just sitting there, like I didn't give them specific instructions. Please God, tell me why.*

After mediation and several deep cleansing breaths, I worked up enough strength to get myself together to address these two wonderful parents as I exited the bathroom aka my private confession booth. Careful to keep my composure I asked *"WHY ARE Y'ALL STILL SITTING HERE?* Ok, so maybe I didn't actually yell at them as the all caps would imply, but in my head I was screaming.

They both responded as if they had no comprehension of the English language spoken upon drop off. "*I don't know,*" these two 60-plus-year-old humans replied. "I don't know?" I snapped back. My blood began to boil and the lid began to shake. "Where did the lady that I gave the money to go?" I asked.

"I don't know," They repeated. Did my mother let me give that woman $30 bucks to park her and my stepfather in front of that door? She must have thought I was a fool for real or made out of money, because why else would they let that lady leave without taking them to the gate? So here we are, me, my mother in a wheelchair and my stepfather on wobbly crutches. I'd managed to find another, more trustworthy, airline escort to help get us to the check in point, yet pride forbade Mr. Leroy to accept the assistance of a wheelchair. Instead he'd insisted on a one-crutch strut through the airport. My mother held the other.

We managed to get to the TSA without further incident—or so I thought. Mr. LeRoy, who'd failed to inform the agent that he usually got flagged, set off the alarm because of the metal plate from an injury sustained in the war. My mom and I made our way through with no issues, and as we walked through to the other side of the checkpoint, Mr. LeRoy was standing there with his khakis down around his ankles and arms stretched out in his multi-colored jacket and green shirt! First off, why did he look like he hadn't any family? The pants were too big; he was wearing at least five separate colors and nothing matched. At this point I began looking for the camera crew to pop out cause I just knew I was being punked.

As funny as that airport story is, it took me a minute to see the humor. It's now that I really can laugh without crying. The behavior my mother demonstrated on the return trip home was the catalyst that God used to provoke the change by which I would forever view my mother's behavior.

Traveling back to Maryland was no easy feat, and to add insult to further injury my mom's sister, Aunt Nancy, accompanied us, as she wanted to spend a few days with my mother. Aunt Nancy was my mom's baby sister. She was nothing like my mother, and her words of comfort during my pregnancy reminded me that, despite disappointing my family, God still loved me. Her words: *"That's why God put erasers on the end of pencils. Everyone is entitled to make a mistake."*

While in the airport we'd been informed at check-in that our flight would be delayed. Great! I thought to myself, I had time to canvas the other gates in search of breakfast for everyone. It was an early flight home, and both my mom and Aunt Nancy needed something to eat so they could take their medications. Mr. Leroy was chilling as usual, not bothering anyone for anything.

After I'd taken the orders, Aunt Nancy and I headed to Burger King. On our way back to the gate, we heard the announcement that our flight would be boarding soon, so we hurried a bit. It was Aunt Nancy who realized that our order was incorrect and my mother insisted that I take it back and get what she'd ordered. I did my very best to explain that there wouldn't be enough time for me to do that and make the flight. But it was as if a switch went off when she heard "no." She exploded with anger and hate spewed from her lips. I shrank from embarrassment, hurt, and anger, wishing to be anyone other than myself. Mrs. Leola called me every name she could think of, except Charlene Ransom. That car ride from Maryland to Philadelphia was a long, quiet one. After getting them settled, I drove back home to New Jersey. That night I dreamt, and awoke even more disappointed than I had been in the airport. I'd worked to get past those feelings, but after traveling, I found myself back in that dark place: a scared, 14 year old girl. Angry, I prayed.

That Sunday morning as I was leaving church, I ran right into Dr. Patton, Director of our clinical support group. On the verge of tears and unable to formulate words to describe my mother's actions, her harsh and cruel words now triggering the worst in me, I approached Dr. Patton.

"I had that dream again!" I said trying to sound normal.

"What dream?" Dr. Patton questioned. She looked at me with that soft gentle smile on her face, her head tilted just slightly.

"Of me killing my mother."

"Charlene," Dr. Patton began, "Now you have been in school long enough to diagnose your mother." She continued, "Now tell me what would your response be to a client, sitting in front of you?"

I wasn't expecting that response, but as my mentor I have always respected and trusted her advice. Her words forced me to think and reconsider not only my emotions, because they are mine and I owned them, but to look at my mother's behavior in a more clinical manner.

Being able to diagnose my mother was a defining moment in our relationship. I no longer saw her as just my mother, but as a patient. This forced me to consider not "What have you done?" but "What has happened to *you*?"

TIP "If we want to understand the oak, it's back to the acorn we must go." – Oprah Winfrey. Being trauma informed means that we can't just focus on the poor or problem behavior; you need to understand the root cause. "It's not what did you do?, but What happened to you?".

Dr. Patton helped me to see her through a therapeutic lens, which allowed me to stop being a victim. I hadn't learned about the trauma-informed care modality just yet, but had learned enough to know that Mrs. Leola was unable to be the nurturing mother I craved, as a result of her trauma-filled life. Historical trauma, domestic abuse, and many other adverse experiences had prevented her from being the mother I needed her to be. For many reasons, my mother was unable to support my emotional needs, therefore when analyzing her behavior, variables such as a traumatic past, a culture shaped by trauma and collective trauma needed to be factored in. I could no longer *just* see her actions; now consideration had to be given to the root cause of her behavior. I was more inclined to meet Mrs. Leola where she was, which allowed me to be more empathetic and mindful of who she was without forcing her to be what she was unable or maybe unwilling to be—including my mother.

Trying to change people to fit your needs will always fail.

When taking a seat, you approach a chair and sit with trust and faith that it will hold you, because that's its job. More often than not, you sit with confidence having a foreknowledge from chairs you have previously sat on. However, the next time you sit, the chair lets you down because you fail to notice that one of the legs was broken, only realizing its unsteadiness when you fall. You get up, disappointed in the fact that the chair is unable to do its job. Now here is the revelation; if you go back to sit on the same chair, you can't fault the chair. If it wasn't able to support you the first time, sitting again in the same chair with the fractured leg and expecting it NOT to fall is an unrealistic expectation. However, the peace of mind you can walk away with is that the chair is still a chair, it is just in need of repair.

8

"If you don't let the past die, then it won't let you live." Author unknown

ONE YEAR, MY best friend, Terri, and I planned a trip to see Cathy, a friend of ours who attended North Carolina A & T college; it was homecoming weekend. At the time, I was living on my own as a single mother and was looking forward to a great time with the girls. I'd arrange for a coworker I'd befriended to stay with Mikey. I hadn't told my mother of my plans and didn't feel the need to do so because—let's be real: I wasn't beat to hear the fifth degree from her. She was a master manipulator and would have asked every question one could possibly think of right down to the color of my undergarments, if it meant she could have control over who was caring for her grandson. Nevertheless, everything was set and we were on our way. Terri shared our plans with her mother, Mrs. Barb, and gave her Mrs. Leola's information in case of an emergency. To my surprise, my mother also had Mrs. Barb's contact information. When we got to North Carolina, Terri called her mom to tell her that we'd made it safely. I listened as Terri's mother spoke on the other end. Mrs. Barb was so upset. I could hear her voice shaking as she described the events that had ensued. She said that Mrs. Leola had telephoned in regards to my whereabouts. The two women had never spoken prior; so to hear second-hand of my mother's berating as it pertained to me was enough to leave anyone rocked. Mrs. Leola's words that day, *"Tell Charlene she could lick my vagina."* I'm sure she used the *"p"* word, but Mrs. Barb was too much of a lady to repeat it. Through the phone I could hear Mrs. Barb repeating *"I don't know how a mother could say such things about her child."* My mom was mad that I hadn't shared my weekend plans with her, and the fact that Mrs. Barb knew pissed her off even more. Terri tried to calm her mom down, but neither myself nor Terri was surprised; we knew that was how my mother spoke every day, especially to me.

That was the first time I had seen someone express genuine concern and speak up to my mother on my behalf. When I was younger, I'd always wished someone would just call the cops or protective services—or even Ghost Busters for that matter—to come and rescue me from the wrath of Mrs. Leola. Here I was in my early 20's, a mother myself and made to feel as if it was mandatory to give an account of my comings and goings.

Through tears Mrs. Barb told us how she told my mother that she would never speak to her child like that and couldn't believe she talked about me the way she did. Mrs. Barb never knew how her sticking up for me made me feel.

When my mom learned of my pregnancy, I was in my eighth month. The year I graduated high school I'd spent the summer at Cheyenne pregnant. No one knew I was pregnant, and it wasn't until that November when I came home for Thanksgiving that I hadn't just gained a few extra pounds, but in fact, I had a live *turkey in the oven* according to my dad, due December 31st, 1985.

However, there was no nostalgia for Mrs. Leola, who immediately sent me next door to a dear friend's house, Shirley, who was like a big sister. Every chance I got I would escape to Shirley's house during my teens. At Shirley's, I could come and go as often as I wanted. My mom respected Shirley because she was a strict Christian or "Holy" as she would often say. Shirley spent time with me, taking me to church and on shopping excursions.

"Go see Shirley," my mother instructed. I don't know why she wanted me to go see her, maybe she thought Shirley was going to be disappointed in me which would prove, I guess, that I wasn't worth all the consideration or love that Shirly had shown me over the years. In fact, whenever I had done something wrong in school, or anything she would call up my uncles and aunts and tell them how awful I was. Maybe she thought Shirley in all her holiness would be ashamed or something. I don't know, but I went and Shirley was the big sister I needed.

When I walked into the house, Shirley already knew. I don't know how, but she did. She hugged me, as I cried. After a few moments or so I'd managed to muster enough strength to ask Shirley to come with me, as I planned to tell Mrs. Leola. Together we walked back to my mom's house and shared the news. I wish I could tell you it was a simple *"Charlene is pregnant by Louie"* and be done with it. But no, my mom asked many questions and wanted to know every detail: the time, location, color of socks I had on, etc. The interrogation was awful. According to her, I was the worst person in the world. She kept yelling, *"And you said you weren't going to be like Sister!"* I had sworn not to be like my sister in that if I was going to have children, I would be married, or at least that's what I thought.

My mother could be bitter, angry, and cantankerous at times. The sad truth is, she was *that* way more often than not. Mrs. Leola tried to beat the baby out of me and when that didn't work she offered my child to relatives down south who didn't have children. I felt that I had no say, and really thought she would make me give my child away. After about two weeks, Mrs. Leola stopped soliciting family members in search of adoptive parents. I'd never planned to live with my mother after I graduated high school, yet there I was crying and convinced I would be stuck with her forever—although not having a plan or even the means to move out didn't stop me from dreaming of what life could be for me and my baby.

The best part about that Thanksgiving weekend was my family, who visited from New York and North Jersey. Mrs. Leola was usually the host, her temperament tamed for family. My family and extended family would come through our doors like it was their home. My mom often provided a room for anyone who needed a place to live. We had four bedrooms and the one guest room was commonly known as the "*purple room,*" which many occupied for weeks at a time.

Ironically enough, my pregnancy was found acceptable amongst present family who seemed to also be supportive, although reluctant and sensitive to the feelings of Mrs. Leola. But somehow God won. It was as if we needed a tension release as conversation seemed to be stifled, given the circumstances. While we were gathered around the table making polite small talk, I'd stood up, forgetting about the little turkey I was carrying; I attempted to *squeeze past* and couldn't. Knick-knacks flew from the table creating uproarious laughter amongst us. Everyone joked as the tension that once hovered had now been replaced with laughs and love—everyone that is, but my mother who was inches away from combusting.

Cooking was my mom's passion. She could certainly cook, and that was a fact! Every holiday, she would make her famous rolls, cheesecakes, coconut cakes, pies, and Lordy Lawd, mac and cheese, potato salad, greens, roast beef, pig feet, chitterlings, and hog mogs—I'm hungry! During the summertime, the one-car garage that never saw a car inside became a dugout for the BBQ. Mrs. Leola would have everything on the grill: chicken, steaks, hot dogs, hamburgers, and seafood. Drinks and soda were in abundance. There was always more than enough to feed the entire neighborhood and I'm certain she did at one time or another.

Mrs. Leola would spend her summer days sitting on our front porch. We lived in a townhouse, and every two homes on our row shared the same stoop. Most times the neighbors would come to our stoop and sit and talk for hours. Some nights if my brother, Charlie, was outside with his friends we were permitted to be outside with them. Our stoop had a whole vibe, from neighborhood kids seeking love and freeze pops from my mother's stash of treats to the day-to-day knowledge of Noblet Ave. This one particular day, Mrs. Leola and Mrs. Carmichael, our neighbor, got to fussin'. Mrs. Carmichael lived a few doors apart, with Mr. Harry and Mrs. Shirley in between; everyone could hear them. About what, I really don't know, but what I will never forget are the words Mrs. Carmichael shouted across the stoop to my mother, *"You ain't nothing but an old whore, laid up with two different men!"* My eyeballs must have looked like saucers as I listened and waited for what I knew was going to be the clap back of the century. Mrs. Leola sat on the stoop unbothered; I watched her from the bottom steps as she hurled her hate for only Mrs. Carmichael to catch, *"You just mad you don't have anyone over there licking your black ass."* And just like that, Ms. Carmichael headed back into her house. Now don't get me wrong, I don't condone the words used, but I absolutely have so much respect for my mother who, on many occasions, showed me that you don't let anyone shame you for being your authentic self. I wished I had understood that as a child, or even as a young adult. Heck, I was probably well into my 40s before I figured that lesson out.

9

2 Samuel 4:4 (Jonathan son of Saul had a son who was lame in both feet. He was five years old when the news about Saul and Jonathan came from Jezreel. His nurse picked him up and fled, but as she hurried to leave, she dropped him and became disabled. His name was Mephibosheth.) NLT[6]

IT WAS JANUARY 15, 1981, and I was 13 years old. My big sister, Loraine, was taking me to Washington, DC to join over 25,000 other Black Americans in protest, declaring January 15th, the birthday of the late Reverend Dr. Martin Luther King, a federal holiday. As excited as I was about *this* protest, sadly enough it wasn't my first time *protesting*. After the middle school in my neighborhood closed, we had to go to Folcroft Middle School, an all-White school in the next town over. Our parents, commissioners and other concerned citizens of Darby Township attended meeting after meeting to fight for our community school to remain open to no avail. Folcroft was just under two miles from our house, and according to the zoning laws it was too close for busing. To get to school we had to cross State Highway Hook Road, a four-lane state highway, without a crossing guard to safely see us to the other side. I don't remember much about the first school day, but I do remember the events after school. While we all walked home from school, men on trash trucks threw bottles and other debris at us. Terrified, we all ran home as if our lives depended on it—because it did. Sometimes you can just feel things. We just ran, not watching for oncoming traffic, and didn't stop until we had all crossed Hook Road. It was only by the grace of God that no one was hurt on that day. There was no conversation from any of us kids. I remember running through the front door and straight up the steps to my mom. Out of breath, I managed to get out what had happened; her ears heard my words and the fire flamed from her mouth. She began to call her friends and many of them happened to be those same people who had been fighting for our school to remain open. By that night they had a plan and they gave us very clear and precise instructions on what we should do when we returned to school the next day. They told us to wait until the last few minutes of class to individually get up and walk out of the class to go down to the main office. Once we got to the office we were to sit on the floor or on the chairs, but we should refuse to leave the office until the school provided us with a police escort home. Meanwhile our parents were planning to contact the school district and the local media to bring light to our issue.

The next day we followed their instructions to a tee; each of us leaving the classroom a little at a time to go to the office. We began to fill up the empty seats and when the seats were full we began sitting on the floor. The secretary kept asking what we wanted and no one said a word, until the principal walked out to see why the office had become what looked like a seating area in the airport after a flight had been delayed. I don't recall who spoke up first, but several of us responded to the principal's question with *"We can't leave until we get a police escort home for our safety."* The school office began to fill with teachers coming in and out, some coming in for what appeared to be their mail, but had trouble navigating a clear path without stepping on us kids. Others just came to be nosey, but quickly exited at the sight of us. I don't even remember the principal's name, but he went back into his office flustered, and though it was clear we were not leaving, he asked at least two more times for us to please leave the office, because the staff needed to go home. I remember asking, "Isn't our safety important?" I'm sure he replied yes, but he would not call the police.

To make matters worse, the police station was directly across the street from the school. It would have taken less than two minutes for him to call and them to respond, yet no one came for hours. It was around 6pm when the first officer walked into the lobby of the school. We could see because the office had ceiling-to-floor windows. After speaking with the principal, the officer walked into the office and asked us to gather our stuff; he assured us that we would get home safely. Fear of the police was just as real as fearing the neighbors in the community, but we knew our parents had reached out to the news and if something bad happened to us at least it wouldn't go unnoticed or unreported. We did as we were instructed, and walked out into the dark that awaited us. The police did follow us in their cars as we walked home. Only two cars escorted us, and when we got to the end of the road that met Hook Road, they stopped and we ran across the street as we had done the day before. I can't speak for anyone else, but the fear was just as real and my adrenaline was running wild! We didn't get home that night until after 7pm!

It was so early that it was still dark outside when we got ready to leave. My mom had packed the cooler with ice for the sodas and my sister had me load up the car with packed sandwiches and snacks for the drive. We were probably on the road for no more than 20 minutes before I was asleep.

"Next exit we stoppin' to go to the restroom," Loraine announced to everyone in the car. *"Charlene wake up, you got to go to the bathroom?"* As I opened my eyes, I tried to figure out where we were, but couldn't. I didn't recognize anything but my sister's voice and

thought to myself *"Punk, I ain't sleep."* Sassing back was something I never did. Nor did I use derogatory language or raise my voice in front of my mother. I didn't dare utter those words for fear of having my head knocked off. Lorraine's bathroom PSAs not only interrupted my solo radio performance, but also my sleep. I'd been drifting in and out of sleep since we'd hit the road. When I wasn't asleep, I was singing along to the radio, just the chorus though; I hadn't learned to memorize whole songs yet.

"Come on, we are going to the bathroom." Lorraine urged me out of the car and into the rest stop.

Before I could get out I had to get back into my snowsuit. I had taken my topcoat off and rolled it up to use as a pillow. But they were leaving me, so I said *"bunk the coat"* and hurried out the backseat to catch up to Loraine and her friends. It was January and the temperature was brrrrrr cold, but I didn't care one bit about how cold it was. I had on layers of clothes to keep warm; the energy was electric and enough to keep me awake despite my sleepiness.

The youngest amongst my sister's friends and our cousins made me feel like I was so cool because I was hanging out with my big sissy, and my mom was nowhere around to fuss, yell, or hit me! It was so exciting to be hanging out with my big sister. I idolized her; she was the coolest person I knew. Once we arrived in DC and parked our car, she made sure I didn't get lost in the crowd. We walked for what seemed like hours. The weather, once no longer a concern, had now grown colder and with every new step I struggled to keep my feet from crumbling and to keep my hands warm. The crowd kept moving, and we kept up. Everyone was chanting "Feet don't fail me now." I guess I wasn't the only one with frozen feet, yet despite the cold, we understood the assignment at hand: to get to the mall to hear Stevie Wonder. We had a mission to accomplish and that was not up for debate or compromise; I didn't mumble one complaint, and went with the flow of the crowd.

As we got closer and closer to the stage I remembered thinking about what I heard about Woodstock in school: how massive the crowds were and how free-spirited everyone was. Everyone was so loving and kind to each other: no issues with race, just people: Black, White and other nationalities walking and marching for the same cause. I wondered if that was the same experience we were having in DC. It felt like everyone was family and friends. There was so much love and positive energy that it felt awesome to be a part of such a historic moment and I was right there in the middle of it all.

Eventually we made our way to the Washington Monument. Outside, the temperature was freezing, but that didn't matter. The excitement of waiting for Stevie Wonder to take the stage was enough to warm us, along with some random jumping up and down. Although there were many guests who came on stage, such as Diana Ross, Martin Luther King III, Gil Scott-Heron, civil rights activists Ben Chavis, Dick Gregory, and Jesse Jackson that day, none received the welcome Mayor Berry of Washington, DC did at the time; he was booed off the stage as he attempted to address the crowd: *"If we [Blacks] continue to find fault with each other,"* Marion Berry began while a slow booing began to brew amongst the crowd. Mr. Berry continued his address, his voice now straining to overpower the chants for him to leave the stage. *"We will never be able to fight the bigger issue: racism and equality for all."* The crowd continued their boos even louder than before. A defeated Marion Berry exited stage left, at which point the crowd began chanting again. This time for Stevie Wonder. Knowing that Stevie would soon be on stage, my sister grabbed my arm and pulled me behind her to move closer to the stage. We stood right down in front, but right beside the speakers, which were taller than I was. My ears felt like they were going to explode from the blaring bass.

We moved in even closer, and just like that, he was right there on the stage front and center, Mr. Stevie Wonder. He began to speak, "As an artist, my purpose is to communicate the message that can better improve the lives of all of us." He then asked a roaring crowd for a moment of silence to honor past civil rights activists who were no longer with us. I looked around to see masses of people who with bowed heads and closed mouths stood still in a spirit of unity to honor Dr. King and the others. As Steve Wonder began to sing his version of "Happy Birthday" the crowd, as if cued, began to sing along. Together we sounded as if we'd been in the same church choir, only these members were of all hues and were filled with love, joy, and peace. This moment was the reason we had all come to DC on what would have been Dr. King's 52nd birthday. I would remember this day, this feeling, forever, as it would be the foundation on which my desire to advocate for social justice would be built.

Before I knew it, we were back in the car headed home. We arrived home in time to see the concert that was planned to celebrate the birth of Dr. King on television. Later that evening as we watched the special hosted by Stevie Wonder, my godfather came over in the midst of my recapping of the day. My mom loved Chris. He would come over often to hang out when my sister was in town visiting, or just to come and eat some of my mother's home-cooked meals. When I was ten years old or so he asked my mother if he could be my godfather.

Excited to see him, I sat in the living room, but he didn't see me—or at least it felt like hadn't. Instead, he followed the smell of marijuana and the sounds of laughter to the second floor of our home, where my sister and mother were hiding. The sounds of muffled secrets followed by uncontrollable cackles trailed through the vents to our middle school ears as we struggled to decipher their language, wanting to laugh too. These visits proved themselves beneficial, as Mrs. Leola had little time to reprimand me; her mood was much calmer, her words less aggressive.

Finally everyone had settled; my mother was tucked away in her room with her door closed. My sister was asleep in the guestroom, my brothers were in their bedroom and I was on the couch. I had probably fallen asleep waiting for everyone else to go to sleep. I can remember Chris sitting next to me as if we were on a date. In my mind, he was my boyfriend, although I knew 14 was not nearly old enough to have one and if I did; a boyfriend would probably be more around my age. Chris was at least 24 years old, certainly not age appropriate to be my boyfriend. The longevity of our "relationship" was enough to deem us a couple, at least in my mind. By now Chris and I had been seeing one another for I guess three or four years, a secret I vowed to myself to keep, along with others. Chris was never aggressive, nor did he force me; he just manipulated me and used my ignorance to get what he wanted. There was never any sign of abuse. It began with fondling and it wasn't shocking or strange, in fact, it felt familiar. Let me explain why: I had seen pornography, and though I had never engaged in intercourse, my body would respond to what I saw. So when Chris touched or kissed me, those very same feelings I felt emerged, and yes, they felt good. Eventually he would use his mouth on my vagina, and often kiss me while his hands fondled my breast and vaginal area. On this night he would be no different, at least that's what I thought. The room was especially dark, except for the light from a muted television. Anxious and nervous, I waited for him to make the first move as he always did. His hands had touched parts of my body before. I didn't see him as a predator; I thought he loved me, and what we had was special, though tonight didn't feel special; it felt so strange. As we sat on the sofa kissing, his hands slid into my pants. He always guided my hand to touch his penis through his pants, but this time he unzipped his zipper and opened up his pants. My heart raced, uncertain of what to do because he had never taken off his pants before. I thought about telling him to stop, but I thought he would be mad and not want to date me anymore. My father always showed pornographic movies in our house but this was different.

Despite having seen pornography as often as I probably watched cartoons, it wasn't what I thought happened in real life. I was so scared that I would do something wrong and he would find out that I wasn't as mature as he'd thought and break up with me.

Suddenly the hall light came on and panic set in. I couldn't imagine what my step-father would have said if he'd seen me and Chris on that sofa. For sure he would have had no choice but to tell my mother, and there was no question whether she would leave me alive long enough to explain. Chris stopped kissing me and his hand stopped moving. Stilled by fear, we listened hard to what sounded like footsteps making their way downstairs. Then the footsteps stopped and the sound processed in the opposite direction. He turned around and went back up the steps. The hall light went out. I don't know if he forgot what he was coming downstairs for, or if he thought my sister was downstairs with someone, but he stopped, and went back to his room. Nevertheless, I don't know how far things would have gone that night. I just know that I was never so glad to have been interrupted at that moment—not because I was afraid of getting caught, but because I was happy not to be forced to go even further, because I was in no way mentally, nor physically ready for intercourse.

TIP Child Molestation Vs. Sexual abuse. Child molestation generally refers to a single or isolated act of sexual assault against a child. Child sexual abuse, on the other hand, refers to a pattern of sexual abuse that persists over a period of time. Child molestation is also only used to describe a sex crime against a small child, such as an infant, while child sexual abuse is more commonly used to describe sex crimes against older children and adolescents.

When I was about 10 Chris started placing my hand on his penis. On at least two occasions that I can recall he attempted penetration.

I cried both times because it was so painful. He would kiss and tell me it was ok, and reassure me it would get better. I remember thinking that it was painful because I didn't know what to do, especially since the women in the porn movies appeared to enjoy it when the men put their penis inside of them. And, given that pornography was my only sexual reference, I'd conceded to that being the reason why it hurt so badly. I didn't know this was abuse until I was in my early 30s. Had Mrs. Leola known what that man was doing to me, I have no doubt she would have attempted to kill him herself.

Kissing and fondling was bad, but it didn't hurt. I liked how it felt when we kissed; I didn't understand why my body neurologically responded. Chris knew I was naive, and he used that against me. He also knew my mother trusted him with me and he used that against her. Chris was in the Navy, one of the reasons my mother would allow him to take me and my brothers swimming at the Philadelphia Shipyard. For good reason, my mother was afraid for us to go to a pool or to be around bodies of water without proper supervision. Chris would exploit her fears while preying on her child. He would ask to take us to the pool to "teach" us how to swim; however, I don't remember him teaching my brothers; he mostly stayed in the pool near me.

TIP: What are the signs of a child predator?
Gives gifts or special privileges for no apparent reason. Overly affectionate/playful with children—hugging, tickling, wrestling, holding or having a child sit on their lap. Disregards "no" "stop" or other efforts from a child to avoid physical contact. Long stares or periods of watching a child.
The sole characteristic all child molesters share is having thoughts about being sexual with children, and acting on those thoughts. These individuals actively seek access to children and the opportunity to be alone with them.

Chris returned home after being stationed in Japan for several years and announced he was getting married. I was devastated and felt betrayed. "*Getting married,*" I thought, how could this be when I thought he was coming back home to get me? I began to run through the possibilities of things I could have done wrong to make him want to marry someone else. Confused, I began to think I lacked whatever it was she had, which made me feel that my lack of sexual experience was the reason why he "broke up" with me. I was in my late 20s when I'd see him again after getting married, and he still tried to sleep with me. Despite the years of sexual abuse, the emotional and mental control he continued to have over me, I entertained the idea and him being married to someone else didn't bother me one bit, because unfortunately, the damage done so many years prior had rooted itself in my self-esteem and confidence. The years of abuse were now surfacing by way of impulsive sexual behavior with men. After a few days of thinking about his request as well as my needing to prove that I was woman enough for him, I invited him over to the house I was sharing with my father. My son was visiting my mother. My father was spending the night with his girlfriend and there was no reason to worry about being caught.

As we lay there in my bed he kept asking what I thought were stupid questions, despite what former teachers encouraged me to believe about there being no stupid questions; his were. He pressed me about using drugs and tap danced around the passing of a drug test; it was the strangest exchange, because I wasn't doing drugs. And I definitely didn't understand how it would have affected him if I were. While he attempted to kiss and touch my breast, I felt dirty, much different than I'd anticipated and I didn't understand why. As a teenager, I used to think of the words I would say to him when I saw him again. Words that would somehow comfort the feelings of dismissiveness that lingered given his new commitment; I wanted to know why he hadn't proposed to me, why he didn't think I was worth marrying. I needed to dispel the feelings of inadequacy that festered around my sexual inexperience because I believed that if I had been a better kisser and had known how to please him, he would have loved me enough to marry me. None of that happened; there was no eruption of euphoric emotions, instead only disgust filled my soul for the person lying next to me. No longer did I have the need to ask him anything, nor did I desire to prove my worth. I found his presence loathsome, but certainly not to outdo the stench of alcohol that now permeated the room. For sure I was going to have to open a window and light an incense when he left. His tongue in my mouth was nauseating. And, as he now lay beside me I knew he was nothing more than a predator and never a boyfriend. We never slept together that night. He left, and despite my rejecting his advances, periodically, he continued to pursue me over the years.

10

"The past cannot be changed. The future is yet in your power." Unknown

THE PHYSICAL ABUSE had stopped, but because Chris was a part of my extended family, there was no doubt that I would see him and maintain a strained relationship limited in communication on my part. However, he was very persistent. He continuously sent me messages through social media to which I would respond with one or two words. Eventually I blocked him and stopped responding to him altogether. As time went on, I realized that the interactions Chris had with me constituted abuse.

In 1996 I was invited to a support group for victims of sexual abuse at my church. As one of the ministers in training I thought I was being invited to the support group to help serve the ministry. Talk about divine intervention. God had a different plan in mind. His providential nature is to already have the answer even before we are ready to ask the question. Honestly, I didn't understand at the time why I was there, and for the first few sessions I felt like I was hoovering as these women shared their stories, that in some uncanny way became mine. As I listened, reality set in and although I lived in denial for some time, learning the pattern of a predator and hearing the testimonies of the others helped me to come to terms with the truth. I had been abused. Shame and guilt probably weighed more heavily on me than the weight of the secret I had kept for so many years. Taking back the power he stole from me required me to first acknowledge that the "relationship" I believed so much in was in fact sexual abuse and a lie, which wasn't easy because I still thought it was my fault. Even after years of counseling, I struggled to say I was abused. I certainly would have never told my mother! She would have spread that information like a wildfire in the Nevada desert. I don't think I would have ever survived that.

As a teen I never told my mother, because I didn't want to get in trouble for having a boyfriend, not because I felt she wouldn't have believed me. And, by the time I was an adult I knew that if Mrs. Leola were to find out she would turn the experience into a circus, with me balancing on what I thought was the truth. I also didn't want to have to face family and friends, because if she knew, everyone else would know too, which would leave no way to get around the looks of shame. I wasn't ready to face that kind of judgment, nor was I ready to respond to the dozens of unasked questions around why I didn't tell sooner—or even those inquiries questioning my level of intellect. There was no way of coming back from my being sexually active, let alone my believing that Chris and I had been in a relationship. It wasn't until I spent time in the support group that I understood that my silence was a trick used by the devil to keep me mentally bound and isolated with my own distorted perceptions of the incident. Years later I discovered that my brother, Charles, knew. I told my sister, Loraine, and I regret ever telling her. She confronted him. I don't know what her purpose was in telling him, nevertheless the secret was out and there was no way to keep it covered any longer. My sister's betrayal hurt me deeply, and it was her inability to keep a secret that was the reason for not being so open with my family in the first place. I was angry about that for many years. My trust in sharing was destroyed and I vowed to never be that vulnerable again.

Loraine's role in my healing was to support me in the work I'd been doing while in counseling, yet her confronting him undermined that, and instead I felt as if she'd taken my confidence and handed it to him on a silver platter. Ironically enough it forced my hand at exuding courage, as I would have to face him again. Confronting my abuser was something I hadn't had the courage to do for years. I never saw myself saying no to him. He stalked my social media and would send me messages asking when he could come spend the night and when was I going to invite him to my house for dinner. He tried over and over to convince me to let him come to my home. I knew I would never have him in my house no matter how convincing he tried to be. As a child, what I remembered about his persuasive and manipulating demeanor was that he could conveniently convince me to do what he wanted, and I obliged, conditioned to do nothing else. I was more worried about how telling my secret would not just impact my family, but I was also overly concerned about his as well, while ignoring my own self and emotional well-being in the process.

Holding that secret and not telling anyone for years was a huge emotional weight. I felt ashamed; I thought it was my fault that I didn't know that what he was doing—and had done to me—was wrong. I felt embarrassed for years at the fact that I had allowed him to even be a part of my life for as long as he was, even after becoming an adult. The wonderful news I can share with you as you read this is the liberty I felt the first time I admitted that I had been sexually abused. It was far greater than holding the secret. For years, being alone with my secret gave Chris the power to continue the abuse as he continually tried to work himself back into my life. When I was finally able to share, I realized that God had strategically placed me in that ministry to receive the love and encouragement I needed. The great thing about support groups is you're not obligated to share. I could sit and listen, and even provide words of encouragement to those who shared. It's still not easy to say, but as the evangelical preacher Joyce Myers penned in one of her books, "DO IT AFRAID!" I found a safe place to finally break the silence in the support group.

> **TIP** Avoidance coping—also known as avoidant coping, avoidance behaviors, and escape coping—is a maladaptive form of coping in which a person changes their behavior to avoid thinking about, feeling, or doing difficult things.

When I was in my 40s I confided in Terri that I'd been abused. She was her usual supportive self. She didn't ask me a million questions or even push for more information. I shared and she listened. Empathic and genuine, her words reminded me that his behavior was not my fault. We had been talking about my failed relationships, and I was struggling to figure out why I was unsuccessful in maintaining a healthy one. At the time, it felt like a cycle of repeated behaviors all ending with the same result and I couldn't understand why. They say insanity is doing the same thing over and over and expecting different results. I was expecting different results, but was clueless on how to change the pattern.

Please see the list below for reasons why people don't immediately or ever tell that they have experienced a sexual assault.

- Shame: Even though sexual assault is NEVER the fault of the victim, often those who experience it feel as if something is wrong with them for having experienced it. If you are ashamed of something, you are less likely to share it with others.
- Fear: Fear of not being believed, fear of retribution, fear of how others will react to you and treat you, fear of how

police will respond, fear of being ostracized, fear of being judged. These are just some of the types of fear that people may feel when thinking about telling someone what they experienced.

- Uncertainty: People who experience sexual assault may not know they have rights. As a result, they are less likely to know what they would be required or not required to do if they disclose that they were a victim. They may not know that they don't have to report to the police*, or that they don't have to have a rape kit if they don't want to. People may also be uncertain whether what they experienced is assault. Some people don't recognize a sexual assault as such until someone else points it out to them.
- Guilt: Sometimes when people experience sexual assault they go over the incident in their head again and again, trying to make sense of what happened to them. Victims may blame themselves, which leads to feelings of guilt. And like shame, when someone believes they are guilty of something, it is difficult to tell others about it.
- Avoidance: It is not uncommon for people who have experienced sexual assault to want to forget it happened and "move on." They believe they can do this by not thinking or talking about what happened. Additionally, talking and thinking about a traumatic experience can be painful, thus, people may avoid this at all costs.[7]

Being Face to face with Chris I was as scared as a 13-year-old little girl about to get caught kissing on my mother's sofa, but I was 51 years old. He was sitting in my car in the passenger seat and talking like he was catching up with an old friend, telling me about the things he had read on my Facebook page, and asking about my relationships. Then the conversation took a turn and so did my tone as I became angry at his justifying his behavior. I listened as he tried to pacify me and quell the storm that was obviously brewing.

Then, out of nowhere, he blurts out *"Why did you tell your sister I abused you?"* as if I was the violator. I sat still as his words fell hollow through my car; he tried to make me feel guilty for telling her. The air seemed to leave the car, and words danced around in my head as I struggled to compile a response, feeling more like a shaken salad than anything else. *Why wasn't I supposed to tell that secret I asked?* Was it really something special between just me and him? I thought to myself. Absolutely not! No. He was still trying to manipulate me to get what he wanted by implying I had no business telling Loraine about our "relationship."

I sat looking at him, reflecting on my distorted perception of his actions. It was not a relationship; it was abuse. I remembered the misguided feelings I'd had for him and the many secrets I'd kept in an attempt to keep private what for sure should have been disclosed and dealt with by my parents and the authorities. "*Someone should have advocated for me,*" I thought. Memories of what I know now to be manipulated attempts to break my spirit and steal what was never meant for him made me angry and filled me with a rage. My heart broke for young Charlene and the shards I wanted to use as weapons, but the grace of God interceded, and the Holy Spirit spoke. *"What if someone touched your 10-year-old daughter as you did me?"* I watched him closely, not wanting to miss a word. His head was down, but not like he was ashamed of his behavior, he was still trying to manipulate the situation. He replied "*You were so mature and I thought you liked it.*"

His words were nauseating. Disgusted, I now saw him for the pedophile he was.

He saw nothing wrong with his actions, and implied I was at fault for its continuance. The more he spoke on the matter the more he disclosed his interactions he'd had with his children's former babysitter. For a long time I felt guilty that I didn't know that what he was doing to me was wrong. Although I knew his behaviors weren't my responsibility; I couldn't help but think that if only I had known better then, I could have possibly prevented him from harming another child. It was liberating to take my power back, similar to the first time I disclosed the abuse during a counseling session. As a result of speaking those words out loud I had gained the courage to not bend to his will, which was something I hadn't only done with him, but also with other men as I seemed to attract men that never honored my "no" and were skillful at convincing me to give into their desire while they ignored mine—something I judged myself harshly on, as I believed it to be a weakness. Fearing rejection, which was the typical outcome, I succumbed to their advances. Despite telling him he was the cause of the emotional trauma and the reason I had such a convoluted perception about intimacy, he showed no remorse and normalized his behavior. I knew he would no longer have access to me, yet somehow I didn't feel free from him as his presence at family gatherings seemed almost intentional.

During the summer of 2019, I received news that one of his nephews had died. Instantly my heart began racing, and the feeling of nausea overwhelmed me as panic set in at the thought of attending the funeral. Why did I even care? I didn't have to attend. Besides, both my parents and his mother had passed away, so I really had no reason to go, yet I knew I couldn't not go. I needed the courage and strength to go and act like he was not even there, a huge test. And I trusted God to get me through it.

I was working as a Lyft driver trying to make a few extra dollars for a trip I was taking. I had a fare in the back seat and we'd become lost while also to find her drop-off point. It felt like we'd been driving around for hours, when the phone rang. It was my sister, Loraine. I answered frustrated, convinced the doctor's office we'd been looking for didn't exist as we drove around and around this complex looking for the location the passenger kept reciting. *"Hello Charlene! Guess who died?"* She was hyped up and talking fast; I had to ask her to repeat what she was saying.

"*Chris died,*" she said flatly. I still hadn't found the office, and needed to drop off the passenger. I could not find words to tell her to hold on, or that I would have to call her back. I just held the phone. The voice from the passenger jolted me out of the fog that filled my head and thoughts. It took everything in me to not break down and cry. It was just strange. Like wow, I just asked God to give me the courage to even be in this man's presence, and just like that *he was dead*. The swallowing of guilt and unspeakable joy had begun to escape through welled eyes. As the car door shut, the pressure within my chest tightened more, now that I was left alone with the news. Through blurred vision I drove, uncertain of where I was going until I found myself in front of a Wawa, sobbing. I was happy...and shamefully guilty for feeling so glad about that. He was dead. There was guilt in my mourning, yet there was a peace that left me weightless for the first time in a long time. I wanted to cry, but I couldn't; I wanted to shout, but I couldn't. Her words echoed and I listened in disbelief. "God you really do love me. I spoke to Him. It was as if God was saying I need not fear or worry about being intimidated by his presence any longer, and simply removed him.

I praise God for Chris's death and my freedom. I wouldn't ever have to speak to him again, nor would I have to figure out how to navigate chance meetings at family functions. Hallelujah! He was dead, and I was so grateful to God for being true to his word. The adrenaline from years of abuse and hiding were beginning to take over, and my hands shook as I searched for my phone to call in prayer reinforcements. Watching the steady flow of traffic and listening to the monotonous sound of unanswered rings was a much needed distraction. In need of an outlet to process and spiritually place the grief I was feeling, I called Terri, because she knew all about the abuse I had endured. Not once did Terri push for details nor did she ever share my story with anyone else. Next I called Assata, my line sister. Being able to share this with my sorority sister was surprisingly easy considering we had only met four-or-five months prior. That day, God used her to speak life into me, reminding me of God's love and favor in my life.

My mother trusted this man; she thought he would keep me safe while I was in his care. He dropped me metaphorically and damaged me emotionally, and for years it negatively impacted many of my relationships. But God! Like Mephibosheth from the Bible, I was now summoned to the King's table, not for what should have been a death sentence, but for the extension of grace and love given by King David.

TIP: Promiscuity and sexual abuse don't make good sense but at the same time, they do. It does make sense that someone who has experienced sexual abuse as a child would deflect from relationships because it's a way for them to be in control. Research shows that this is not always the case. Victims of childhood sexual abuse can engage in promiscuous behavior. They also struggle with emotional intimacy in relationships.[8]

As an adult, relationships, as you can imagine, were somewhat of a challenge. And, not ever having had the full relationship experience, courtship included, made it difficult to navigate the authenticity of potential suitors, which often left me broken and hurt in my own regret. Naivety reigned in all facets of my decision making, and allowed me to believe their status lies of singleness when in reality they weren't, and misunderstand their actions for reciprocity. I longed to be in a "relationship" that was indicative of those romanticized on television, in movies, and of those I'd read about. I wanted that love. And, I wanted it publicly, certain that the years of being shrouded in dark corners of basements were no more, and the phoenix Charlene that was arising would settle for nothing less than a Met Gala Monday experience seven days a week. Unfortunately, most times I ended up with no love, and with concern for myself that I'd again misread the conversation and misunderstood the "intimacy." Most times the men that pursued me were of the same predatory nature, telling me what they thought I wanted to hear. There were also those who were just interested in the sex, as a junkie is interested in the next fix; all they had to do was persist and my no would become yes, even if never spoken. It took me well into my adulthood to understand that sex does not equate to love, and that my no means no. Being a survivor of sexual abuse left me in a fragmented state of overanalyzing, self-doubt, failed relationships and a lack of confidence that over the years I would work to successfully piece together in order to partner with God in recreating me.

11

"The paradox of education is precisely this – that as one begins to become conscious one begins to examine the society in which he is being educated." James Baldwin

BECAUSE I STRUGGLED with academic concepts, learning had always been a challenge, especially reading. I remember always getting in trouble while at school for distracting the class in the hope of being asked to leave because I didn't want to be called on to read aloud. I'm certain Ms. Smith wanted me to learn, but I just couldn't catch on to what she was teaching. So instead I became the behavior student and labeled the class clown. But it didn't start there; my classroom antics began way before middle school; I believe it was nursery school when my privileges of sugar cookies and chocolate milk were revoked as a result of restlessness on my part. I would try to fall asleep like my classmates, Debbie or Lisa, because when they woke up they always got the afternoon snack. If only I could behave and fall asleep on cue like the other kids. Instead, I used our quiet time to fall out of my chair to make the other kids laugh as *they* drifted off to sleep. It was only after they awoke that regret set in, leaving me jealous of those who'd made the juice and cookie cut for afternoon snack. Sometimes I managed to remain seated at my little desk, keeping my hands to myself, but something would happen and giggling would ensue, leaving me again snackless. Every day I would remind myself to "be good tomorrow" but somehow would end the day upset with myself. As much as I hated classroom instruction, I did love going to school because it was a way to escape the toxicity of home, where I felt restricted while living under a cloud of heaviness that certainly didn't foster a desire to learn and grow. If my mom got a bad report from the school, she would punish me by making me write something out of the dictionary a hundred times, and if that wasn't enough, she would then make me take that same writing to school in the hope they would equate to a credit for a missing assignment. I would be forced to read books and submit reports which were always interesting to read considering my lack of comprehension and decoding skills; the story details were always a bit skewed, but entertaining nonetheless. It was hard because if I didn't know the words I was reading, I certainly couldn't give an accurate description, because what I understood was questionable.

Learning shouldn't ever be a form of punishment. Another revelation that came to me while taking a developmental psychology course on how teachers can help to foster a love for learning, just in the way they set up their classroom. One year I was a substitute teacher in Ms. Jay's kindergarten classroom. Ms. Jay also had a co-teacher, however on this day she was absent. The enthusiasm she had was just amazing to see in action. Her room was staged with various free-play stations and the walls were brightly painted, making it a very inviting classroom for young minds to learn and grow. There was a medical station with a stethoscope, a little white lab coat for the doctor to wear, and other items for the children to play with. In the kitchen area was a stove and a table and chairs, along with food and dishes. There was a reading center that I quickly passed on, making my way to the center that held all things family and home related. One by one the students came in for the morning, each putting their belongings away in their cubbies, and after checking in for their daily routine of attendance and breakfast, they each went to their preferred center for free-play.

As I stood imagining my own free-play, I couldn't help but be a little envious of the learning these students were exposed to, revealing to me how the combination of resources and love helped to shape these young academic minds and hearts—something I'd missed out on. And, judging by my commitment to experience every station, I certainly would have enjoyed it. Ms. Jay kept them engaged, and did so fuss free. There was sharing and gender inclusion, as well as the freedom to be as they rotated, allowing everyone a second turn. When the final timer sounded, they each began to clean up and gather in the reading center: my dream bedroom. There were books on little bookshelves that stood about three feet high. Bean-bag chairs were slouched in corners where little stuffed animals in small baskets sat waiting to be read too. It was the coolest reading area I had ever seen, and young Charlene was taking it all in. Ms. Jay and I sat in the center of the floor with the students. She held what looked like a small music box. Inside the box were pre-printed name cards of each student. I watched each child burst with excitement as they waited to see who would be selected to choose the first book to be read. It was just awesome to see how something I hated was presented in such a magical way, so that the results were conducive to the environment. I felt so excited that I wanted to read too. Before I knew it my hand was raised like the others in the hope of being selected to make a book selection. Ms. Jay recognized my enthusiasm and selected my erratically waving hand. I don't remember the book, but I remember reading it and using a range of voices for the characters as they presented themselves. The kids laughed, and some would fall over laughing like it was the funniest story they had ever heard. For a moment, I would travel back in time to where young Charlene sat in my first grade teacher, Mrs. Greenhouse's first grade class, except more confidently. I was as excited to read aloud as every other student in the classroom. For over 40 years I had worn the label of "*Unable to Learn,*" but that was a lie, and that day I proved them all wrong.

By this time I had graduated college, so I certainly didn't have the issues with reading I had as a child, but I think that day I found a love for reading because of that teacher's presentation and ability to meet those little scholars right where they were. Mrs. Jay made learning fun, interesting and full of energy. I only spent one day in that grade level, but it was the most memorable experience I had had in a classroom, and it made me want to teach. I wanted to be the kind of teacher that made students desire to learn, to explore and grow. I wanted to be able to make it simple enough that regardless of their level, the students were able to understand.

Like Ms. Jay; my 6th grade teacher, Ms. Allen, also made learning fun as she incorporated interactive projects in her instruction. For example, we did a health project and I was the model for the life-size drawing we used to discuss the human body and how to care for it with healthy foods. I loved going to *Studevan Middle School*; it was much different than Folcroft Middle School. Almost all of our teachers were African American, and so were the students. Unfortunately, I still got into just as much trouble. However, Ms. Allen, my English Language Arts teacher, was a light. After receiving an A on an essay I'd written about Christmas lights and the true meaning of Christmas, she encouraged me to submit the persuasive writing composition to a local newspaper. With the help of Ms. Allen, who walked me through the submission process, I did, with great excitement. To the surprise of us all, it was good enough to be published in the Delaware County Daily Times, *"Do Joy and Love Need Lights"* by Charlene Stuart. I remember how proud my mom was of me. She made sure to get copies of the newspaper to share them with family members in New York and our family in Virginia. I still have that article in my home library.

The experience with Ms. Allen was a stark contrast to how I felt sitting in other classrooms when teachers would call on students to read out aloud. When my turn was coming up I would get sick to my stomach, anxiety ridden over who the teacher would call on next. Often, I'd put my head down, praying that I would be skipped over. But as if I had a neon sign over my head blinking "Pick Me," the teacher would call my name and the dread of stumbling over words overcame me. There were also those times when the teachers felt that everyone should read, and like a military drill sergeant, they would go down each row of desks monitoring tone and enunciation. When they'd heard enough, a motion was made for the next student to begin the next section. I didn't like that either. Most times I'd lost my place trying to keep up while also trying to figure out the section I would be assigned. I could never pre-read to prevent snickers and jokes from my classmates, which left me feeling somewhat defeated, because I always wanted to read as expected and on cue.

Another one of the Studevan greats was Mrs. Watkins; she was older, and one of the sweetest teachers. She, like many of the African American teachers at Studevan, understood that the history of African Americans wasn't fully shared in the books offered, and made sure to incorporate our history in the lessons they taught. For example, we learned about the Emancipation Proclamation and how president Lincoln freed the slaves, but for two-and-a-half years after, many Blacks remained slaves; this was one of the many historical facts NOT taught at Folcroft.

Mrs. Watkins was short, with short curly hair and she wore eyeglasses that slid down on her nose. I remember getting kicked out of her language arts class daily for being silly and clowning around during instructional time. After a few months of routine kick outs, Mrs. Watkins and I had established an understanding, in that she no longer told me to "get out" when I was clowning around and disrupting her class; instead, she would ask me to "step aside." Instinctively I knew when Mrs. Watkins had had enough of my foolishness; she would hold her head down, and look over her glasses and what came next was the most polite removal I'd ever experienced. Sometimes, I would make a plea to save myself "Mrs. Watkins can I just ask..." but she never let me finish. It was probably for the best. Defeated in my attempts at remaining *in* the class I would solemnly make my way to the desk she'd stationed right outside her door, where I would complete the day's assignment much better than if I'd stayed in the classroom. I drove her crazy every day, but one thing is for sure; she loved her students and never gave up; neither did she give up on us.

Mrs. Watkins also, like a few of our teachers, lived in our community, and once told my mother that I sent her to the altar every Sunday. When my mother told me I was really beside myself and put Mrs. Watkins right with all the other teachers who'd told lies on me. And the fact that my mother would potentially believe her over me was even more bothersome. I remember thinking *"Like seriously, how was I sending her to the altar on Sundays and we wasn't even in school on Sunday?"* I was so done with Mrs. Watkins—until I realized what an altar was. The poor woman was covering me with prayer. She saw potential in me and spoke to God on my behalf, only to confirm how God has always had angles around me covering and protecting me. That's what I call being favored by God, and not because I was special, but because He trusted me to fulfill His purpose and be an ambassador for Him.

High School was different for me; I didn't hate it as much as I did when I had to transfer to Folcroft Middle. The greatest lesson I learned while at Folcroft was learning how to discover the "can" in "can't". One of the best things that happened to me in school was being invited to join the Key Club and taking part in the Toastmasters International. I was in 10th grade and just excited to be doing something outside of the special education classroom. By this time I was utilizing my ability to memorize words. Sometimes I may have just learned how to spell the word but on occasion I may have even known the meaning. But that didn't matter. I was able to learn this new skill of public speaking and I was good at it. At these club events, I was able to participate in public speaking and impromptu speech contests with students from other schools. It was like the Miss America pageant for academics. When they got down to the final contestants, the host asked a question and gave each contestant two minutes to respond. I would watch and listen as each participant replied, and then listen to how the commentators dissected their answer. The key to impromptu speeches is to be versed in current events—not so much to be an expert, but to be able to engage an audience as you speak to inspire, motivate, and persuade them to believe your initial claim. I would come home week after week with another blue ribbon, having won another competition. It was so much fun, and I guess my commitment to watching World News nightly, and never missing an episode of 60 Minutes every Sunday night paid off.

Despite the label placed on me in the 7th grade, my struggles with reading, and even the ridicule and shame I felt from my classmates, I found confidence in myself.

12

"Only one woman is able to love a man more than she loves herself. It's his mother."

I DON'T THINK I really gave much thought to having children when I was growing up. My sister had three children who spent the summers at our house, which meant I had to watch and care for them—while under my mom's supervision of course. Sometimes I would take my niece, who was just 10 years younger than me, everywhere, which was pretty much nowhere since the town I grew up in was small; we had but one bus that went through two or three neighboring towns. However, there was a McDonald's on the bus route and I thought I was a whole grown adult on the bus to Darby, PA. Watching my sister's children was an opportunity to get out and not be stuck in the house living on pins and needles. My niece and nephews were beautiful babies and I loved doing their hair and getting them bathed and dressed. We would go to the park, to drill team practice, or over to a friend's house to escape the daily routine of watching soap operas. I probably should thank her for giving me an opportunity to enjoy summers instead of being young and restless while spinning in the world as it turned.

Although the summer days were spent watching my mother's "*official and unofficial*" grands, the time spent allowed me a glimpse of what parenting might look like. And I wanted NO part of it. However if the miracle were to happen, I knew for certain I would rather have a son than a daughter, because my niece would scream like nobody's business: scream like at-the-top-of-her-lungs scream, soul-piercing-octaves-for-no-reason screams—not to mention the "daughters" my mom had adopted over the years; those chicks had about three children each.

I also didn't date, which helped to prevent the possibility of my having a boyfriend. Though becoming pregnant soon put that into perspective, as it was a shock to both my family and friends. Heck, it was a shock to me. Louis, my son's father and I were really good friends. We certainly weren't dating—or at least I didn't see it that way. Louis made me comfortable in his presence and I never felt like he tried to persuade me to do anything. Unlike Chris, Louis asked if he could touch me, kiss me, see my breasts. He also asked if we could have sex. And, when he did, I said yes.

TIP Distorted view of self and relationships: Good self-esteem begins in babyhood—with parents who respond to your cries, make you feel safe, look at you with affection, smile at you, hold you, comfort you when needed, and make you feel loved.

Parents who allow you the freedom to explore, are there to pick you up when you fall, make you know you can depend on them, and don't tell you what's wrong with you.

In fact, good self-esteem grows from a safe and secure environment—meaning safe and secure parents who see who you are, are proud of you, support your strengths, and help you when you're struggling: parents who believe "you can do it!"

These are parents that never violate your safety or boundaries. When you don't have those kinds of parents then you learn there's no one to trust.

Louis and I hung out every Friday night before I left for college. My uncle MC would come from Media, Pennsylvania, to sell my mom and his 50/50 tickets from the Holy Cross Church. I would run out the front door and around the side of our house to his, which was just one street behind ours. I remember never having to knock for entrance and always feeling welcome. Miss. Carolina, Louis's mom would make sure of that, with hugs and a warm welcome. I knew she loved me. And, I loved her. Miss Carolina would be upstairs in her bedroom, or sitting in her living room watching television. I would hand her the tickets and she would reply, "Louie's downstairs. Go head *down*," and I'd make my way towards the basement door before she could finish. In the basement, we'd listen to music while talking and just chilling out. We laughed about everything, and I looked forward to it, because it was one of the few times when I could go out without feeling anxious. My mom didn't call to ask if I was still where I said I was going be, only to tell me to come home, because she trusted him and his family. And I trusted him too. He made me feel comfortable and he was never inappropriate. I definitely didn't see him as my boyfriend, which is funny because when everybody found out I was pregnant no one could figure out by whom, let alone how! Shortly after my parents found out I was pregnant with his child, Louis became my "boyfriend."

When I had my son, I wanted to give him more than what I had had as a child, and by that, I don't mean material things, but a different kind of childhood experience. I didn't want to be demanding or hard on him just because he was a boy, but I also knew there was a need to avoid being soft, because the world for him would not be kind, confirmed only by his beautiful brown skin. I also knew it would be important to have good role models, of which there were slim pickings amongst the folks I knew. There was my brother Charlie, but he had his own adverse trauma history and was in no position to offer parenting support. His way of dealing with his trauma was self-medicating with street drugs. Michael, my younger brother became available as we got older, but he, too, had his own set of challenges raising his children.

Monday, December 30, 1985, at approximately 7 pm: The "cramps" started. Unaware of what to expect with contractions, I assumed cramp because the pain in my belly was similar to that of a menstrual cycle cramp. Typically, my cramps were strong during that time of the month. So much so that growing up, I would go to the school nurse to lie down, to which she would oblige without incident. Except one time the cramps were so bad that the nurse, unbeknownst to me, called my mother for permission to administer pain medicine, which was an epic fail. Not only did I not get relief while at the nurse's office, but once I got home my mother cursed me out for even going to the nurse. After that, I never brought my cramps up again, and when I felt the cramps that night, I just figured I'd go lie down, and suffer in silence as I had done before.

Lorraine was at my mom's this week for the Christmas/New Year break. She went into my mom's room and called for me. I was in my room, adjacent to hers, lying down. I got up and walked into the bedroom, and for some reason decided to sit down on the floor in search of comfort. Lorraine began questioning me about why I was in bed so early, about the kind of cramps I was having, how long they were lasting and when they had started. She went on and on, while my mom looked on, knowing all the while I'm sure. By this time it was closer to 10 pm when Lorraine declared, "Oh my God, you are in labor!"

Lorraine called Eric, her son's father, who was downstairs, to come quickly because *Charlene's in labor!* He ran up the stairs and stood at the door like he was planning to deliver the baby right there. I sat on the floor exhausted and in need of sleep; I also wanted them to get out of my face. Unfortunately, sleeping was not in my foreseeable future, it was *show time*. And in pure dramatic fashion, Lorraine went about the house rushing in and out of bedrooms screaming *"The baby is coming! The baby is coming! The baby is coming"*

Quickly, they got me up from the floor, while someone got the little bag that my cousin-sister Elsie had brought for me to take to the hospital. She'd given me everything you would get at a baby shower. My mom hadn't allowed me to celebrate having a baby with a shower, but Elsie had brought so many baby clothes and other necessities that when Michael came home, we didn't need or want for anything. Elsie purchased a beautiful oak wooden crib that my brother and Louis put together. They rearranged my furniture and placed his crib in the corner where my bed had once stood and filled it up with all the clothes and diapers and baby stuff he would need for months to come.

As Eric drove with me *contracting* in the passenger seat with my sister in the back, I heard my mother's last words; *"I hope you feel the pain I felt when I found out you were pregnant."* Good thing the ride from Sharon Hill to Chester Crozer wasn't far, or at least it didn't seem far considering Eric drove at the speed of light. Eric kept saying *"If the cops stop us we just gonna point to you and say a baby is coming."* We pulled up to the front entrance of the hospital, and before I could maneuver my seatbelt undone my sister was out of the car *helping*. I managed to walk into the emergency room, where a nurse, upon seeing us, beckoned for a wheelchair. I was taken back to a bed where after being examined it was determined to be a false alarm, and was informed of my discharge. The team that had welcomed me in had dwindled, and a lone nurse delivered my discharge papers, and just as I got ready to walk out of the room, my water broke. Michael must have said "No ma'am, I need to see what's going on, so here I come." He was born December

31, 1985, on his due date, making his entrance into the world perfectly timed.

Labor was long. The night faded; daytime was on the horizon and I was miserable, as the cramps got worse. When the epidural was offered, I'd refused. I wasn't feeling that needle in my back. I'd much rather chew glass. However, around 8am that morning and after having been in labor for nearly 12 hours I'd made a frantic attempt to revoke my epidural "No" to a solid "YES," but it was too late. Instead, I was given something intravenously which made me sleepy.

"*The baby is turned around*," Someone said. And, just like that, chaos ensued.

"We need to get him turned, he isn't breathing" said a voice, although I couldn't tell whose. Over and over I'd receive instructions to push and not push and then push again, before they realized he wasn't coming and the pushing wasn't working. Finally, the doctor declared that an emergency C-section was needed.

Meanwhile, my sister had gone to call my mom, while the two nurses and the doctor began to physically push the baby into a delivery position that wouldn't compromise us both. The nurses present pushed on my stomach; one straddled the table while the other stood. The doctor was also on the table pushing while we all rolled on the gurney to the operating room. The scene was intense, even for me, and was largely reminiscent of a movie scene. I began to think that I would never have sex again if it meant not going through *this* level of pain. Exhausted, and wanting the ordeal to be over, I pushed one last time as my sister and cousin Roberta stood anxiously looking on. The whispers filled the room, which was when the doctor began to explain that in order to get the baby out an episiotomy was necessary. As he talked, he cut, and with the use of a suctioning device and forceps a delivery occurred. After unwrapping the umbilical cord from around my baby's neck, a cry filled the air. I looked down at this little human, nestled up against my chest, just under my chin; my eyes could see his little face covered in what looked like slime (what I now know to be the embryonic fluid). If the slime wasn't shocking enough, his skin was a purple hue. I was guessing he was struggling as much as I'd been. A small gasp escaped me prompting the doctor to explain that my baby would be in an incubator temporarily, but would be released once his color changed, which, if I was lucky would occur over the next few days. As the nurse walked away with him, I blurted out his name: Michael Terrel Freeman.

I've heard mothers say that the pain they experienced during childbirth faded once they laid eyes on their newborn. Now I don't understand how they forgot, but let me just tell it like I felt it. The cut that doctor made, I felt. The tearing from Michael being pulled, I felt. He was 36 years old at the time I am writing this book and yes, I still feel and remember that pain! If that was what my mother meant when she told me she hoped I would feel the same pain she had felt, well, I felt it—and I don't wish that pain on anyone, not even my enemy. Medically I had complications from that childbirth; subsequently, I have had two surgeries to correct the damage since then. I jokingly tell Michael he is still my pain in the butt—pun intended.

After delivery, I became sick and was unable to see Michael for the first day or two. When the nurse finally brought him to my room, he was so small, I thought that if I wasn't careful I would break his little body and my mother would kill me for sure. I also didn't see myself in him, but for sure he resembled his father; both had the same little cone-shaped head. Michael was now able to sleep in the hospital crib next to me. His little head was full of curls that framed his face, and his fingers were long. To myself, I thought he'd either play basketball or piano. And, believe it or not, he's a musician and plays the piano. Michael was healthy and happy and didn't cry much. While in the hospital I tried to breastfeed him, but was unsuccessful and conceded that if being a breastfeeding mother was the secret society of womanhood, I wouldn't earn a membership card because childbirth and breastfeeding weren't for the weak. It was clear to me that I was weak, as the process of breastfeeding was tortuous, and after a few attempts of what felt like someone trying to remove flesh away while tearing my soul, I kicked that idea right out of my head and requested the medication that hardens your milk. I might not have known all it meant to be a mother, but what I did know was that I loved being his mother and I wanted to be the best one I could be. I didn't know how or even exactly what I needed to do, but I knew I wanted him to know he was loved, and that I was his biggest cheerleader.

Having Michael changed my entire world. I had someone who needed me as much as I needed him. We grew up together. Some days I failed, and other days I succeeded. I worked hard and tried to provide the best for him, which often meant riding on buses to jobs and traveling back and forth to school on public transportation where the commute was two hours one way.

Over the years, I struggled to keep apartments, which forced Michael and me to move around a bit, because my income was barely enough to make ends meet. Sometimes we stayed with Mrs. Leola. Although the living arrangements seemed to work for Mikey and my mother, I felt like I was always anxious and on edge: a constant reminder of growing up in her home years prior. I felt restricted, and often moved through her home like I did when I was a young child, cautious not to disturb anything and quiet enough to hear her when she woke up. I couldn't fully be his parent because my mother, despite my being an adult and paying rent, attempted to parent us both.

Mrs. Leola watched Michael for the first six months of his life. Every night I would gather everything together he would need for the next day for my mom, and every night she would curse me out about something and threaten that she wasn't going to watch him in the morning. Frustrated, I would reach out to a few people who'd offered to watch him for me, should I ever need a sitter; fortunately for us, finding a sitter was never a problem. But like clockwork, every morning as we prepared to leave my mother would insist that I leave him and not take him out in the cold weather. After a few last-minute cancellations with the sitter and never wanting to be indebted to anyone, I decided to no longer rely on my mother's indecisiveness and instead began to take him to the sitter each morning, then I'd make my way to the bus stop.

Michael did so well at the babysitter's house. He had other children to play with, and Ms. Myrtle began to introduce table food to Michael. She taught me how to prepare the food so he would eat it for me at home. For instance, she showed me what a little banana mixed in with mashed potatoes would do for his appetite. Ms. Myrtle saw no wrong in the children she cared for, and never would she allow me to call him bad. She always said he is a boy and that's what boys do; let him be.

Ms. Mrytle taught me how to parent in a way that was unfamiliar, yet it felt right and I was most grateful for the opportunity and time spent with her. Raising a boy into a man was not an easy task. Being in the church was a saving grace for us both, as I depended on God to guide me in raising him. I have been both his mother and father, and despite fulfilling both roles, I knew I couldn't teach him how to be a man. However, equipping him with the right tools to be successful when he grew up was paramount. It's funny how sharing this chapter with him has helped to enlighten us both on my parenting style. He said that had I given him the charge of being prepared to provide for or lead his family, he might have been more focused as a teen and could have spared himself from the pitfalls he'd experienced as a young adult. What grace I was given to have been able to have that conversation with him. I wished I had the opportunity to go back and share more with my parents in such a way that I, too, would be able to say sorry for judging them as harshly as I did while growing up. We finished that conversation with me explaining to him that despite how I raised him, he has become exactly who God intended him to be: an amazing father and provider, all of which he was before having his own children.

When Mikey was growing up, I didn't trust many people around him because I subconsciously thought I would be exposing him to the possibilities of abuse and I didn't want that to happen. If a coach invited Michael to his house after a game, believe me, I was going right with him.

As Michael grew I enrolled him in sports; he played on traveling football teams, and in other sports leagues during his off season. However, football was his first love; watching him play was mine. It took great planning to get to the field early enough to get prime parking so that I could watch the game from the car if necessary. I was that mom who almost never missed a game. During football season I would freeze my buns off watching the game from the sidelines, and in the spring I would be sneezing my head off as I sat watching his softball practice. When he wasn't in either game I would run back to the car to warm up.

Despite the many challenges of being a young single parent—and there were many—it never stopped me from trying to give him the best I could. After being homeless and living out of my car, I learned to balance a budget enough to sustain an apartment for Michael and me, which ultimately led to my being able to purchase our first home in New Jersey in 1999.

13

Church

"Satan desires to sift you as wheat, but I prayed for you..." ~Luke 22:31

IF I COULD have known half the things I'd experienced over the years, I don't know if I would have survived, except for the grace and love of God. The year I gave my heart to Christ and accepted salvation, I was just trying to live a life that was pleasing to God and raise my son. Michael and I had been living on our own, and he was about four years old when I accepted Christ. I did not need much convincing when it came to understanding how God loved me, and wanted to be in a better place spiritually and mentally while having the financial means to care for us both. I knew in my heart God loved me, because of the small things He would do for me. He'd promised to never leave nor forsake me and had proven over and over again that He was Lord over my life, and not following him was not an option. Life wasn't easy when I first got saved. Heck, the very same day I accepted salvation I came home and my brother, after stealing my last $20, ran out my front door like I had stolen it from him. It was a crazy few months, the first few years of my salvation experience was one calamity after another. Within that first year or so, I had everything I owned stolen, I was hospitalized with pneumonia, lost several apartments, and struggled to keep my family together.

But God! Despite having experienced all of that within the first two years of accepting Christ, I was more certain than ever that He is the lover of my soul and my provider. I might have lost possessions, and even some friends during this season, but God was always faithful to provide what I needed daily and it was those times that my faith steadily increased and my knowledge of Him grew more.

When you're faithful in the small things, you're passing the test designed to prepare you for the big things God has in store for you. You may be doing something that seems insignificant, but believe you have much more in you, so don't despise the day of small beginnings. Keep being faithful. Here's the key: We have all been created for a purpose, for some to be a mother, father, teacher, pastor, advocate and such. There have been times while called to assignment that I felt like giving up, and would perform with frustration, discontent and with less than 100% effort. Operating in my purpose requires humility and patience to show up as the mother, the leader, the daughter—or whatever role I'd been designed for at the time—despite the challenges I may have been experiencing. I've mastered the skill of living and learning in the moment, regardless of the environment, and will always use it as a learning opportunity, as even the bad situations work for my good. Complaining about the place I am in won't change it. It's all a part of the process of development. If you complain, you'll get stuck in that mindset, and you will be frustrated and dejected in your spirit, which prolongs what is already a hard place. Walk through the process and absorb everything God intends for you to learn in that season. It was never supposed to be permanent. It's just a step along the way, and just like that, the season will change.

In the Bible, David spent years in the lonely shepherd's fields where nothing happened. It didn't seem like he was making progress, in a similar way to being pregnant—the baby is developing on the inside where nobody can see. In those tough times where you're uncomfortable, you're doing the right thing but the wrong thing is happening; *something* is developing within you that you can't see. It's getting you prepared. You're getting closer to the birth, and if you keep passing the tests at the right time, your anointing will meet up with your purpose. This is the reason many people never give birth to what's in them. They don't understand the process. God will put a dream in your heart. He'll give you the anointing, then he'll send you back to the shepherd's field, like King David, only to develop that which He's put in you. 1 Samuel 16:1-13 NIV. The elevation in your purpose comes later. The way we respond in the wilderness will determine whether or not we make it into our Promised Land. And right now, there are promises that God has put in you. You are pregnant with potential, pregnant with opportunity, with health, with abundance. You've been anointed. I implore you to go through the process to discover your purpose. Will you pass these tests when it's uncomfortable, when it doesn't look like it's going to work out, when you can't see anything changing? Just because you don't see anything happening doesn't mean God is not working.

You don't see it on the outside, but on the inside where it's more important, you're growing. You're developing. It's just a matter of time before purpose shows up!

There's something God wants you to give birth to: something big, something special, something out of the ordinary. He has anointed you for it. The appointing is already in your future. I'm asking you to do your part and be willing to go through the process. Don't let disappointments talk you out of it. Don't let delays convince you it's not going to happen. Don't let the fact that you don't think you're making progress knock you off your square, or keep you from doing the right thing. You've come too far to stop now. You're too close to the birth to give up. It's always the most uncomfortable right before that baby comes.

And the scripture says, "Jesus endured the pain of the cross, looking forward to the joy that was coming." Hebrews 12:1-2 NIV. He endured the pain because he knew it was a part of the process. He also knew that it wasn't permanent. He wasn't going to stay on the cross forever. He kept looking forward to the joy that was coming from the victory in His resurrection. Despite what it may look like, what the report says, what the naysayers are saying about you, you must rest assured, knowing that this is temporary and your promise is to big to forfeit by giving in or giving up!

Don't look back. Don't fall into self-pity. Keep looking forward. The joy is coming. The right person is coming. The dream is coming. The breakthrough is on the way. Stay in faith. Once you're prepared, then God can propel you into your destiny. He can make things happen faster than you thought they would. God anointed David to be a king. He wasn't in a palace. He was in the shepherd's fields. All he could see around him was rocks, dirty stinking sheep, nothing but the dirty grunt work of being a sheep keeper on his father's farm. Your environment doesn't determine your destiny. Where you are doesn't limit what God can do. When it's your time, when you've gone through the preparation process, get ready to be propelled into your God-ordained purpose. Get ready for doors to open that you could not open yourself. Be prepared for the abundance of God's favor in places you never imagined you could go, with people you least expect. God is going to do exactly what He has promised.

Don't get discouraged by the preparation time. Don't quit being your best because you're not where you thought you would be. Friends have passed you up and some have even given up, but that can't stop you. They got married and you are still single, but God hasn't forgotten. They're in a new place. You're still in the old one, but God hasn't forgotten. Keep doing the right thing. Your purpose is coming.

There's a plant called the Chinese bamboo. For the first four years, it barely grows above ground. You can hardly see anything happening, but underground where you can't see, it's developing a massive root system. In the fifth year, once the roots are firmly established, the plant will take off and shoot up to as high as 80 feet in the air, from zero to 80, all in one year. But what makes the fifth year possible is the four years of preparation. Without the years of underground growth, there wouldn't be any above-ground growth.

If it's taking a long time, that simply means what you're going to give birth to is going to be much bigger than you've ever imagined. I read that an elephant is pregnant for two long years. Because the animal is so big, it takes more time for that baby elephant to grow and develop. Elephants typically only give birth to one baby per pregnancy. On the other hand, a dog is pregnant for just 63 days. After two months, the dog can give birth to multiple puppies. There was a story recently on the news where this Great Dane gave birth to 17 puppies, all in one litter. Well, imagine the dog and the elephant having a conversation. The dog says, "I don't think you're pregnant. I gave birth after two months. Something is wrong with you." The dog gets pregnant again and again and gives birth every several months. Nearly two years later, it comes back and says to the elephant, "I'm positive you're not pregnant. I'm sure now. I've given birth multiple times." The elephant says, "No. Here's the difference. The reason you've given birth many times and I'm still pregnant is because what's in me is not a puppy. It's an elephant. What I'm carrying is not ordinary. You don't see it often. I'm carrying something big, something special. That's why it's taking longer."

People around you may be giving birth. They're seeing their dreams come to pass. Be happy for them. But the reason it's taking longer for you is because, like that elephant, what you're carrying is not ordinary. It's not average. What you're going to give birth to is going to be bigger, more rewarding, and more fulfilling than you've ever dreamed. Don't get discouraged by the process. It may take a long time. That's a sign God is up to something big, something amazing. Keep passing the test. Keep doing the right thing when it's hard. Don't run when it's uncomfortable. It's preparing you for greatness! God is faithful to keep His promise and if He said it, I am living proof that He is indeed a promise keeper!

14

"Have not I commanded thee? Be strong and of good courage; be not afraid, neither be thou dismayed: for the Lord thy God is with thee whithersoever thou goest."
Joshua 1:9 KJV

WHILE FINISHING UP the last bit of packing for the Women's Retreat, *Good Morning America* was playing in the background, when suddenly the programming was interrupted by "Breaking News." The female voice began, *"A judge was tragically killed yesterday in Philadelphia."* I ran into the living room hoping it wasn't my judge. Just as I got in front of the television, there it was, a picture of Judge Beryl Caesars; my heart sank. She continued, *"While walking down the street during a local jazz festival a sign that was hanging from a building fell on him."*

"Oh my God, that's my judge." I stood in disbelief.

"He died instantly", she concluded and then casually tossed it to whomever. I stood there with my mouth open, in utter shock as I had just spent six days in his courtroom for a civil case where he was the presiding judge. A few years prior I'd had a nasty slip and fall and the final process after being on Workman's Compensation was a settlement agreement; unfortunately they didn't want to

settle for what I thought was reasonable and we ended up going to trial, which was how I met the Judge. I fell at no fault of my own and had damaged my sciatic nerve, which prevented me from being well for years.

I got up early that Monday morning and set out on public transportation, wanting to get to the Philadelphia courthouse as much as I didn't. I really wanted the entire case to be over, tired of the entire process and wished I wasn't alone. My attorney was there, but he kept trying to persuade me to settle and I kept refusing, because I knew that what was being offered wasn't what I had heard from God. I figured on one number and would have been content, but as sure as my name is Charlene Veronica Stuart Ransom, I heard God say *"What you are asking for, I plan to double!"*

It was the Sunday prior to the trial when God spoke. I'd gone to a neighboring church to hear my Pastor speak at his mentor's church. I hadn't told anyone what my number was, but figured my calculations were less than what the Franklin Mint was offering, because it wasn't like they were trying to do the right thing. I just hoped it would be enough to cover living expenses for me and Mikey for a year. Having to work with only $728 a month often left me short, and I was tired of having to finesse payments each month to still be a payment behind, which added up quickly. Getting help from my church wasn't easy either, because people will judge you for needing help despite the fact they created the systems to help those in need. I would like to add: Just because someone needs help doesn't make them helpless, but that's a different conversation for another time.

So when Bishop Evans said "*God is going to double what you expect from Him*" I was in complete agreement. If God said it, that settled it! The end and AMEN!

After two hours of waiting, Judge Beryl Caesars finally walked into the courtroom and made his way over to the table where I sat with my attorney. He was about 60 years old, maybe older, White, and stood about 6ft 2inches tall. He towered over us, but spoke to my attorney.

> *"Did you tell her to settle?"* He asked. His voice was raspy. "Yes," my attorney replied. He continued. "Did you tell her if she loses, she will not only owe you, but she will owe me too?" Again my attorney replied, "Yes." Judge Caesar spoke again, rattling off numbers and pushing papers in an effort to intimidate me. He addressed my attorney again for what I hoped would be the last time and asked, "Does she understand that's what she'll be responsible for?" "Yes." The attorney replied.

"Yes." Judge Caesar spoke again, rattling off numbers and pushing papers in an effort to intimidate me. He addressed my attorney again for what I hoped would be the last time and asked, "Does she understand that's what she'll be responsible for?"

"Yes." The attorney replied.

As he walked away from the table and headed to his bench, I thought how rude of him, not to even give me the consideration of a greeting—not to mention that the audacity of him to use his power to intimidate me into settling for something that had no direct impact on him was even more menacing. More importantly, he knew nothing about me and had already judged me unworthy of nothing more than what would have been the equivalent of six months' salary.

For five days testimony was given by myself, witnesses and investigators who had been following me for months. They reported my everyday activities like me at the store, the bank and running other errands, and also had video to support their allegations. My going to church on Sundays and as well as other services during the week had even been recorded. It was really a long intense week, but I wasn't worried even a little bit because I heard God say *He planned to give me double what I was asking for*, and on the way to court that morning God said *"Those who put their trust in me, will never be made ashamed."* Romans 10:11-15. And I believed what He said.

As we returned from lunch, my attorney pulled me aside to tell me he had spoken to two people who had been in the courtroom all week, who felt the case wasn't going to go in my favor, and again suggested I consider settling. And, again I refused, especially after the week of false testimony, pictures of the shoes I'd worn to church and time stamps indicating the duration of my outings. I also considered the pain I endured daily which left me stuck and sometimes unable to walk. There was no way I could even consider settling; instead, I politely shooed him away and waited alone in the hallway while the jury deliberated.

It was about 2pm when we got word that the jury was back. My attorney came and found me and watched with hidden doubt as I gathered my things. In the courtroom I watched as the jury entered and awaited my fate. After they had settled, the spokesman handed the bailiff a piece of paper, who in turn handed it to Judge Caesar, who began reading to himself. It was obvious by his facial expression that there was some confusion; he then began to read aloud, confusing me as well. He then spoke to the jury, which prompted the spokesperson to begin reading the decided outcome.

I waited with anticipation to see God show up, and boy did He. Unanimously the jury had decided in my favor and awarded me double the amount I was expecting. It was just as God said, Double! In hearing the awarded amount Judge Caesar slammed his hands on the bench; he accused the jury of not following his instructions and directed them to go back into deliberation because their findings were not in reference to the facts presented.

Not more than 30 minutes passed before we received word the jury was back. I sat there reciting what God had spoken into my spirit on that Monday-morning train ride. Then I prayed, *"God you said if I put my trust in you, I will not be made ashamed. God, I trust you."* I watched each juror walk back into the box and take their seat. Similar to last time, the spokesperson handed the bailiff a slip of paper who handed it to Judge Caesar, who read the paper to himself, before instructing the spokesperson to read it aloud. The spokesman began reading, and again I waited for a jury of my peers to decide, believing that the awarded amount could not be less than double. Because God promised. This time, the awarded amount was three times the amount I'd asked God for. God had done exceedingly and abundantly above it all. I looked down the jury box at each one as the Judge confirmed with an audible reply, smiling with each confirmation. I left the courtroom that Friday and headed back to New Jersey on the train feeling every bit of victory in the name of the Lord. I don't remember crying, but for sure my soul was happy. And I felt that, in that win, God was reminding me of our forever and that His promises for me are true, regardless of what the situation may look like. I couldn't help but wonder if Judge Caesar's tragic death was a move on my behalf. *"Touch not my anointed and to my prophet, do no harm"* Psalm 105:15. And this would be from the KJV.

15

The Procession *"You already have everything you need inside of you right now, today." –Alicia Keys*

IT WAS FRIDAY morning May 13th, 2022: my dad's birthday. My alarm was set for 6:30 am, however, I was up at 6:00, uncertain if I'd even slept the night before. I had laid out my outfit the night before; my fresh-from-the-cleaners white tunic, black tights, and my favorite black sandals. The night before I'd rod set my hair hoping for some nice curls; unfortunately they failed me. Determined not to let failed curls dampen my mood, I began styling and caught a glimpse of myself in the mirror. I saw my mother's face, and knew that both she and my dad would be proud. Overjoyed at the honor of being recognized as *Outstanding Alumnus* at the 54th Commencement Ceremony, I walked into the bathroom smiling and full of energy that not even a double shot of espresso from Starbucks could top.

With my red portfolio in hand, I walked out the door with a full understanding of the day's assignment: to deliver my acceptance speech for being the recipient of the *2022 Outstanding Alumnus of Camden County Community* College. As I walked inside the building for the breakfast reception, I gave the security guard my name, who then directed me to a room down the hall. Walking down the hall, I spotted my Soror and Line Sister, Tjien, and her daughter. About the same time, I received a phone call from my best friend, Terri, who'd just parked and needed to know where to come. As quickly as I gave her directions; the phone rang again.

"Charlene." It was Kelly my photographer. Her voice sounded concerned.

"Hey Kelly," I replied.

She continued on without so much as a breath about the parking situation and somewhat fearful she would miss my big day. We talked Kelly to the right area and waited for her to arrive so that we could walk in together in full entourage style. We entered; there were about 20 round tables, a rack of graduation gowns, and a box of standard graduation caps. Folks were busy taking names of the graduates and shuffling them off this way or that. The graduates did very little to contain their excitement; some squealed in delight, clapping for themselves while others gave high-fives. Their energy was infectious; taking it all in I watched, even more grateful for what the Lord had done in my life.

> "Ms. Ransom," a small voice distracted from my worship. "Are you looking for your Tudor bonnet,?" she continued hurriedly. Tudor? I thought for a moment. She must be talking about the funny little hat I'd been dying to wear. I giggled some. "Yes", I replied. "We didn't order one, but if you'd like you can wear the standard cap." Hmmph, there goes that picture, I thought. Disappointed to not have a picture taken of me wearing the Tudor, I settled for the standard cap, wanting to enjoy this experience from head to toe.

President Borden, the current president of the college, was speaking with a few people as we entered the room, but stopped to acknowledge us. We sat and enjoyed the refreshments, while Kelly began snapping behind-the-scenes photos of me and the other members who would also be marching in the academic procession.

Melissa, the Tudor denier, came over and spoke with my guests; she was giving them instructions about seating just as my sister-friend of over 20 years, Nikki Walker-Brown, came in giving hugs and love. She was extra excited to see that Kelly had, in fact, made it as the night before her attendance was questionable, which meant that Nikki would have to be my photographer.

The room was filling up with more guests, and those selected to take the dais along with me. I stood for a minute taking in the room and the guests, and happened to notice how comfortable I was—as if I was meant to be there. And according to God, I was. Thinking back to my grade school experiences and how hard learning was for me, the feelings of anxiousness began to flood my conscience. Before drowning could ensue, the words of my dear friend Mrs. Robinson came to mind and the waters receded. Her voice in my head was soothing "*Girl,*" I heard Mrs. Robinson's voice clearly, "*You will look back one day and realize you have surpassed them all.*" If only she could have been here for this moment. When Mrs. Robinson passed, it was like losing a part of my soul. She was truly a gift to me.

The former mayor of Camden New Jersey introduced herself and was kind as we shared a moment over our common bond of Commencement speaker, which she had held the esteemed honor of the year prior. Understanding the importance of the execution of the assignment, she offered to cover me in prayer. I was unaware of who Dana Redd was, but in the moment it was a divine meeting; her prayer reaffirmed my position in that space at that time, just as God had.

Melissa, Kelly and I walked to the back of the room where I put on my cap and gown. Kelly took pictures as Melissa assisted with the putting on of the robe as well as strategically pinning on my cap so my locs hung just right. Melissa too, understood the assignment. It was hot under that robe, so I walked around with it open until it was time to line up with the other intellectuals.

Before Melissa and Kelly were escorted to their seats, they'd gathered everything of mine, except my cell phone.

"But what about my speech?" I asked. "I need my speech." I could feel panic brewing from within as I awaited her response.

"You won't need it." Her words were calm in an effort to reassure me. "The speech is on the podium."

"Not to worry," Melissa said convincingly. I reluctantly handed the folder containing my speech over, trusting both her and God that it would be on the podium.

The intellects were summoned to begin the procession. While we waited, Kelly resumed her behind-the-scenes duties and captured really nice shots of me with Dana Redd, the other honored guest, as well as President Bordon, who leaned in during mid-photo and whispered *"You have your own photographer."* Realizing Kelly was with me, he chuckled some and continued, *"Damn, what am I doing wrong?"* President Bordon was a genuinely nice guy. From the first day I shared my story with him, he embraced it and me. In fact, I asked him to write an acknowledgment for my book, and without hesitation, he said yes. Unfortunately, he retired and was unable to fulfill my request before doing so.

We began lining up according to where we'd be seated. I was seventh to be called and stood between Freeholder Louis Cappelli and graduate Denise Diaz who would give the student address. While in line, we made small talk, Mr. Cappelli and I, about his newborn baby and how he was excited to be there, but was being extra careful to not catch COVID-19. I kept asking the name of one gentleman who was processing in with us. I recognized his face, but wasn't pronouncing his name correctly, so no one could figure out who he was. When they introduced the members of Dias, I remembered where I knew him from: Paul Moriarty, New Jersey State Assemblyman, who used to be a news personality on a local network.

By the time we were outside it had started to rain, and like clockwork the support staff from the college began handing out umbrellas. I walked back inside and got one from the many laid across a table, if for nothing else but a souvenir, because that little bit of rain wasn't going to phase me.

We started moving past the friends and families of the graduates, their pride and excitement filling the air. As a former graduate, the procession felt familiar, however this was different, as I was being honored for having graduated some years ago, and for continuing my education whilst being a positive influence in my community. My cousin, Carlton, missed my walk across the stage to receive my Bachelor's degree because he had been late getting to his seat and jokingly told me to do it again. While I waited to walk across the stage, I understood and shared his enthusiasm. Walking across the stage was a big deal, and here I was doing it again. I almost wished Carlton was there to share in not just the walk, but in the blessing of being honored. Silently I gave thanks again. As I walked under the tent toward the stage, I heard a voice call my name, *"Charlene."* I turned in the direction to see a former co-worker quickly seizing the opportunity to snap a picture. It was also nice to see the faces of the young people I'd worked with at Bancroft.

As I continued along the graduation route I heard my name again. I was shocked as I turned toward the voice, only to see a former student from my substitute teacher days, some years ago. My heart exploded with joy and pride in knowing that I must have made an impact on their lives. Seeing students I had worked with, even if for just a short time, made me realize how much I must have meant to them, which made me even prouder to know that my presence in their lives extended beyond the classroom. And those classroom lessons around grief, divorce and life's other challenges were certain to have helped to shape them as young adults, something that I'd never believe myself to have accomplished in someone else. Finally we arrived at our seats, where a ceremonial program with my name, Charlene Ransom sat. It was beautiful. My name was centered in bold, black letters on cardstock. Running my hand across the raised letters felt good and my name looked rich. I'm sure the folks sitting closest to the stage got quite a show, which didn't bother me one bit, because they don't know my story.

The ceremony began and The Board of Trustees conferred on President Borden the status of emeritus, which is a status bestowed upon those who have held and retired from an office, and are given the honor to continue holding the title. Then there was the Commencement Speaker who reminded the graduates of three important facts; unfortunately no one remembers the facts. I was up next, and slid my phone to my lap in preparation. Louis R. Moffa Jr. began by reading the resolution from the Board of Trustees. He highlighted my work in my community and it gave me joy to hear his kind words around my acts of service and advocacy, something I'd been passionate about since my Folcroft Middle School days. He spoke of my academic achievements since graduating in 2005 with an Associate's Degree in Liberal Arts, and touted me for obtaining a Bachelor's degree in psychology from Rutgers University, Camden, as well as an MS in social work from Rutgers University, New Brunswick. As Mr. Moffa continued, thoughts of my mother's acts of service consumed me. Despite her abrasiveness and harsh tongue, my mother served her community and our family. Often, boxes of clothes, some collected and some new with tags, would be stashed away in a corner of our home for families less fortunate than ours. And in the summer, my mother would keep extra boxes of popsicles in the freezer for the neighborhood kids whose parents couldn't afford the ice cream truck.

Lost in the words of Mr. Moffa I thought how proud my parents must be. I stood tall for my mother who had only earned a seventh grade education, for my father on his birthday, for Mrs. Robinson who nurtured me during my winter season, and for the strength of a firm foundation each provided. Overwhelmed with gratitude, I gave quiet thanks for the part each played in creating the woman that stood before many, and for the greatness each saw in me when I couldn't see it in myself. Looking out at the graduates sitting in front of me brought me full circle, and I prayed that they would have the same success and purpose that God had bestowed upon me.

President Borden placed the medal around my neck, and my line sister, Dr. Puge-Bassett, lifted my hair. As the medal lay against my chest I thought it must have weighed about 100 pounds. The front of it read "Bene Merenti," and "Camden County College" on the bottom. In the center sat the school's crest and shield. On the opposite side, it read "President's Medal of Achievement," and in the middle was my name, Charlene Ransom and underneath was my dad's birthday, May 13th, 2022.

My hand slightly brushed across the numbers as I gained my composure while waiting to give my speech, only to be jarred by an unfitting introduction. Mr. Moffa was reading the introduction of another intellect. By this time I had made my way to the podium and wasn't sure what to do. I looked back to Dr. Pugh- Bassett, Broden's predecessor for direction. Aware of the mishap, she nodded for me to remain standing. I did and someone managed to get Mr. Moffa's attention, to which he quickly turned the pages in the book he read from and began reading words and experiences familiar to me.

Before addressing the audience I glanced downward to lay eyes on the speech that Melissa had assured me would be there, except it wasn't. The binder was there, but the words seemed foreign. Mr. Moffa had turned the pages. Panic set in for a moment, but a look back to Dr. Pugh-Basset was the combined preventative and comfort. Meanwhile, a technical superhero appeared while I tried to make small talk. As I began to address the audience, the applause from the crowd served as a reminder that they had not left me, making my heart smile. Unfortunately, the technical superhero couldn't recover my speech either and I was left to fend for myself—something I'd got used to doing in the physical. However, I knew God was with me on that stage just as He'd been with me in that courthouse. And, because He was with me and I believed I knew for sure as the scriptures say, I would not be put to shame, and God's words prevailed.

I began, *I don't think it has ever entered into my thoughts, nor my dreams that I would receive such an esteemed honor. I've sat in plenty of arenas and have listened to many speakers and thought I could see myself doing that. After all, I am a distinguished and competent communicator. I like to refer to myself as a public speaker by nature, but this exceeded my wildest dreams. I am so very thankful and grateful to be here as the 2022 Outstanding Alumni. Thank you to my sorority and line sister Dr. Lovell Pugh-Bassett for the recommendation and Camden County College for this prestigious award. My mother, having only received a seventh-grade education herself, was told when I entered the seventh grade that I was unable to learn. As would any parent, she wanted to see her children achieve greater than she did. So, I can only imagine the disappointment she might have felt when she heard that diagnosis. Her dreams for my life must have felt like sand slipping through her fingers. My academic career has been a journey indeed. I have accomplished far more than many ever thought I would. One of my greatest lessons learned was the discovery of this very small fact. Can comes in Can't.*

I struggled with reading and that made it hard to do almost everything. When my teacher, Ms. Smith, would give me an assignment, I would often reply that I can't do it! She would reply without a second thought. Can comes in Can't. She would say, "Discover what you can do and go from there." I did finish high school, and went on to college. Unfortunately, I failed my first three semesters and was placed on academic suspension. I was sad that I had to drop out, but I was more disappointed that I let my mother down. I was a single parent and I needed to work to support my son. I had to put my academic career on hold, however I was determined to be a college graduate. In 2003 I walked onto this beautiful campus and decided to try it one more time. It was different this time; I was much different and older. Many of the students looked to be my son's age, but I had a mission to accomplish and I wasn't giving up.

In 2005 I graduated with my associates degree and when I walked across this stage I proudly wore those blue and gold cords around my neck. I went on to Rutgers University to obtain my bachelor's degree, and since then a master's degree in social work. Many years ago, someone decided that I was unable to learn, but I am standing here to say—in my Maury Povich voice—that's a lie! Congratulations class of 2022! Someone may have given up on you too! But guess what, YOU DID IT! This doesn't have to be the end. There is so much more for you to do and achieve! SO NEVER GIVE UP! REMEMBER: CAN COMES IN CAN'T; DISCOVER WHAT YOU CAN DO, AND JUST GO UP FROM THERE!

The graduates roared and everyone sitting behind me clapped and cheered. I picked up the paper, folded it back over and handed it to Don.

> He leaned in and whispered "Way to change the atmosphere!" I beamed some. "You nailed it!" he continued. I was proud of myself way more than I ever thought possible. I too knew I had nailed it and the fact that President Borden had said so was icing on the cake.

16

Be not weary in well doing, for in due season we shall reap if we faint not. Galatians 6: 9

AUTHOR MILICENT HUNTER said, *"Don't Die in the Winter."* It's during the winter season that God develops our character so we can handle the blessings and beauty of what God has purposed for us to receive. Typically, the winter months are dark and cold and are most times associated with hardship and tough times that require resilience from those who are to survive. Those that survive in the winter have been nurtured. In her book, Milicent Hunter speaks about the nurturing that seeds receive from melted snow and how the moisture seeps underground and finds its way to the roots. A person's character develops the same way and in most cases during what would be considered a dark season. Like the seed, people are forced to shed away hindrances so new life can emerge which often causes feelings of loneliness and isolation. Don't be dismayed; this is just one season and it has an end date. What God has planned for you will make the winter season dull in comparison. As the perennial is destined to bloom and return every year, you too will bloom. At the end of winter, only the most prepared and the toughest emerge as survivors. Those who survive can declare that they are as resilient as the palm tree.

TIP Individual resilience expands our understanding of stress resistance and adaptation. Increasingly, empirical studies focused on identifying the characteristics of individuals, in particular young people, who managed to thrive despite living in difficult circumstances, resilient individuals have been shown to use effective, active problem-solving patterns.

Living through compounded trauma, my mother had no other choice but to endure her own winter season. She had to do what she needed to care not only for herself, but for her children and spouse. Mrs. Leola, no one could ever say you were weak. You were certainly the strongest woman I knew and lived life the only way you knew how, on your own terms. Your disability forced you to always be prepared. You never let the food run out and the lights never got turned off. We had the same phone number until you died and not once did the phone company have to turn it off for non-payment. You didn't get up making breakfast in the morning before school, but you made sure we had food to eat. You taught us how to cook and to clean. To this day, I still hate cleaning, but actually started a business cleaning houses. It wasn't until much later that I learned about the conversation she'd had with Mrs. Robinson about my business venture. Mrs. Leola stopped attending school in the seventh grade to do day work. She didn't want that for me and told Mrs. Robinson that cleaning houses wasn't a great job. She knew then that I could do better and wanted better for me.

I apologize for not understanding many of the thoughts she had.

17

"A prepared mind favors chance"

IN PSALMS 92:12-15, God said we'd flourish like a palm tree because He knew His people would experience difficult times that would possibly steal our joy, steal the victory in successfully overcoming challenges and steal our destiny right out from under us. And, in order for us to experience the Kingdom of God He designed us in such a fashion that when the storms of life blow, we would like the palm tree to snap right back up stronger than before.

Palm trees have a wide network of fibrous roots that create layers in the soil. These layers hold a tremendous amount of soil which forms an anchor for the tree while enabling it to withstand forceful winds without being uprooted. Even the trunk of a palm tree is different from the average tree; as instead of tree rings, the palm tree has bundles of woody vascular fibrous material. Similar to a cable with lots of smaller wires inside, the structure of the palm tree is more cylindrical than others. The insides of the palm tree allow for flexibility and elasticity. In fact, some palm trees have been known to bend almost parallel to the ground and with amazing resilience, still not snap, and while hunched over under the pressure of storms, the palm tree is actually becoming stronger. The roots are forced to dig deeper and expand further to maintain its anchor. Interestingly enough, the palm tree knows how to flourish during the good times as well as how to weather the storm during the bad. Fully aware of its potential and purpose, the palm tree stands in its strength and during a crisis it is flexible enough to bend and not break.

My character has developed over the years, and having learned how to extend myself the grace to learn and grow, I have used every experience as a teachable moment to become the best version of me. I dislike it when my deeds are mistaken as acts of aggression, or anything outside of the intended good will. If I'm committed to ANYTHING, it's because I believe in it. If I believe in it, then you get 100% of my efforts and passion to see it through. I don't believe in showing up and not being fully present to whatever I am a part of. I bring all of my skills, knowledge, and talent to whatever and wherever I show up. I am one who knows how to maximize opportunities. When faced with a challenge or new projects, one of my top five strengths is being a strategic analyst; I am also known to bring positive and enthusiastic energy to a party, meeting, or any other social engagement.

A few years ago, I was working with an organization as they developed a diversity, equity and inclusion council. The board was appointed to a two-year term, but had already worked together for almost two years before they decided to use a global analytics and advice firm to help the team define the council's strengths and weaknesses. The strengths-finder assessment asked over 100 questions and once completed, we each got a very detailed report that outlined and spotlighted our top five strengths. According to its findings, I am a maximizer and strategic. I possess a unique gift of connectedness, I am positive and an arranger. The accuracy of the results was surprising, and more importantly, read as confirmation for what I'd always known about myself, but was unable to convey in such a way that my strengths would be seen as an asset and not a threat to colleagues and peers. Often, I would be told I was in someone else's lane or doing too much, or I would be reminded of all it didn't take when faced with work dilemmas. For example, during the genesis of the pandemic, I managed a residential treatment program for children with developmental and or intellectual disabilities.

I'd had some knowledge weeks prior to New Jersey's pandemic shut down that what the world was facing was more serious. The folks within my immediate circle thought otherwise and I consistently insisted that this was far more serious than they thought and suggested they not be so passive when considering logistics for our in-person planning meetings. By the time of our first group meeting, we had already learned that the CDC recommended at least six feet of separation from others to aid in preventing the spread of the virus. Managers, nurses, directors, and other team members filled the small meeting space, which felt like we were trapped in a petri dish. In an effort to adhere to the six-foot rule I'd positioned myself in the corner of the room and created a small barrier: my attempt at keeping the virus as far from me as possible given the circumstance. Unfortunately, it wasn't as much of a deterrent as I'd hoped because every time someone entered the room, the first place they wanted to sit was next to me!

The program director began to give the new protocols in the event that one of the residents took ill with the virus, while the nursing staff mockingly demonstrated how to properly put on and remove the PPE. It was as if it was all a big joke to them. The laughing and passive response to what I felt was a very serious situation was ignorant to the science, that should have been most respected by those in the medical profession. It was also becoming clear that the virus and its impact would extend well beyond the two-week timeline given and repeated by government officials. When their demonstration ended, the room became filled with sounds of celebration which just about tipped my boiling point. I'd been watching the news, and to some degree believed the reports.

It wasn't long before the kids, along with most of the staff employed at the group home, became sick. I was out on light duty because of an injury, and was working remotely when I got the first call about one of the individuals showing signs of COVID-19. The kids in the group home are non-verbal and have difficulty communicating when they don't feel well. Their way of communicating is often through self- harming behavior such as head banging or biting. Some have even grabbed a staff member to get attention. Knowing that people were dying and that we were responsible for children who couldn't help us be responsible for themselves was scary. We were the first of the 13 group homes in the program to get sick with COVID-19. But I was ready; I applied every attribute identified in that strengths-finder assessment, and managed the crisis remotely with such a standard of expectation and grace that the director began utilizing my formula when other group homes within our program tested positive.

In a crisis you want me on your team, because panicking is never an option. My group home had a decent amount of cleaning supplies, PPE, and an action plan already in place. I had taken the time to develop the plan in the event that I tested positive and would be absent; whoever was covering could step in and not have to worry. Files were created for each resident containing their emergency contacts and other essential information. I also stocked the residence with what I called my emergency COVID kit: the tote-stored latex gloves, laundry detergent, toilet paper, paper towels, alcohol, over-the-counter medication such as Tylenol, cough drops and Gatorade, for the guys in the home in the event one of them got sick.

My director took the initiative, and set up a meeting with me and several other executives from other programs once we learned that all of the individuals living in the home were positive. Because I had over 10 positive cases it was considered an outbreak, which prompted a virtual rally call to offer support. The call was stacked with heads of programs, the principal from the high school, several members of the nursing team, and a few others whom I don't recall, but who listened attentively while I shared information about the work I was doing with families as well as the condition of each resident. After I was finished, Mark, the director from the adult program said "*Well you should be fine. Everything you have planned is what we didn't know and ultimately was the reason we had such a hard time getting the crisis under control in our program when both staff and clients were sick with COVID.*" Mark went on to further share that COVID lingered for weeks after the initial hit, because the department hadn't got a handle on the spread of the virus. In addition, there was no strategic plan to navigate in the event that someone tested positive. Mark's team had been operating in reactive mode and it would prove to be weeks before they finally came out of that crisis. Now I will say when he said those words, I felt like flexing my muscles just a bit with self pride. I had been trying for weeks to get these same plans in action as a precaution and got absolutely no support from my leadership.

My direct reports did not make it easy to manage the group home during the first few months of the shut-down. The home was a one-floor, four-bedroom, two-and-a-half -bathroom rancher style. It also had two spacious living rooms and office space; mine was in the basement, which also contained a laundry room. During the day, staff from the education team were in the home assisting with virtual learning; the residential staff would come in at midday which created a three-hour overlap each school day; on most days there were 12–15 people working in the residence at one time, making it nearly impossible to maintain the social distance protocol. Staff wore masks when they wanted, and sometimes the rotation of scheduled cleaning of those high touch areas were completed and sometimes they weren't. Conflicts arose between the education staff and the residential staff, each going back and forth about who did what chores and who didn't. The staff wanted to stay in the mindset of what they always did, as opposed to being more flexible in both mind and action now that we were living with COVID.

Apparently, I was *"asking or doing too much,"* according to what I heard amongst the team, which most days left me feeling like an outsider. It wasn't long before the residents and staff were out sick. Worried about their health, I contacted each one of them several times daily for a wellness check, which was emotionally taxing because I was caring for the residents who'd become ill, and I knew their symptoms first hand. The group home wasn't going to manage itself; with the number of staff now out, and I was left with the responsibility to manage; after all it wasn't going to manage itself. Fortunately, everything I had tried to implement months prior was now going to be used with the support of two amazing senior program managers who, along with other team members allowed me to lead them through our crisis. And when it was all said and done, the new system of operation worked smoothly. Reports went back to my director stating how well things went, because right after she ended that emergency *"support call,"* she was out of work for medical reasons, unaware that the staff were all sick. That meant everyone working in my group home had to be sub staff from other programs, and they weren't as familiar with my guys who lived in the house, which could make it a little harder for the subs. But I had a plan of action for that as well.

The sub staff had little cheat cards that gave them a glimpse of the individuals personalities and a list of things they liked or how to best communicate with them. The set up for the house was operating as I hoped, and I was pleased.

For four-or-five weeks, I scheduled meetings with five families and their support teams, to share daily updates on the vitals and the overall morale of the home. The families of the residents felt good that they didn't have to wonder how their child was doing and being cared for because they got to virtually see them daily since they couldn't come to the home to visit. During staffing hours, hot meals for staff were delivered and a staff safe zone to retreat from residents or colleagues was created.

Despite how scary COVID is, and the worry of the families and other stakeholders, we managed it like champions. It was necessary that everyone who would be in that house during that time understood the importance of a team concept. Each was encouraged to consider the feelings of others while I considered theirs, knowing they had their own fears about working in the house with positive cases, as they had families they wanted to get home to, and didn't want to get their loved ones sick.

Conclusion

Charlene Veronica Stuart Ransom

MY STRENGTHS MADE it easy to develop the plan, and more importantly allowed me to prepare for all the variables that would need to be considered, like the education check-in with the education team staffed in the house as well as their program leadership. One morning, a teacher insisted that the education team should provide instruction to students as they recovered, and wouldn't accept my explanation that during normal circumstances when a student is sick the expectation is for them to stay at home; expecting them to perform under our current conditions was inconsiderate. After discussing the matter with the school's principal, he agreed and sent immediate notification to cease home instruction until the students were able to physically return to school. Daily check-ins with the nursing team also continued with specific attention being given to each's symptoms. Consideration had to be given to the disposal of trash, as now trash was required to be double bagged to prevent transmission of the virus on anything discarded. The praise from those who worked in the house during this time helped me to understand how to best operate in my own strengths. I realized that just because someone can't appreciate the value of my knowledge, skills or talents doesn't mean they don't have value. The Bible says that your gifts will make room for you, and in this situation it did just that. Proverbs 18:16 KJV.

In my soul I know that we are all connected. Yes, we are individuals, responsible for our own judgments and in possession of our own free will, nonetheless, we are part of something larger. Some may call it the collective unconscious. Others may label it spirit or life force. But whatever your word of choice, I gain confidence from knowing that we are not isolated from one another or from the earth and the life on it. This feeling of connectedness implies certain responsibilities for me. If we are all part of a larger picture, then we must not harm others because we will be harming ourselves. We must not exploit because we will be exploiting ourselves. My awareness of these responsibilities creates a core value system. I am considerate, caring, and accepting. Certain of the unity of humankind, I'm a bridge builder for people of differing cultures. Sensitive to the invisible hand, I can give others comfort that there is a purpose beyond our humdrum lives. My faith is strong, and it sustains me in the face of life's mysteries.

I am known to be full of positivity, generous with praise, quick to smile, and always the optimist. Some call me lighthearted; others just wish that their glass was as full as mine appears to be; either way, people want to be around me most of the time. I've been told their world looks better around me because my enthusiasm is contagious.

Lacking my energy and optimism, some find their world drab and routine—or worse, heavy with pressure. I look to find a way to lighten the spirit of others and to inject good into every project. You can expect me to celebrate every achievement, and find ways to make everything more exciting and more vital. Some cynics may reject my energy, but I rarely let that drag me down; my positivity won't allow it, although I can't quite escape my conviction of *it being good to be alive, because work* can be fun. Regardless of the setbacks, one must never lose one's sense of humor, which sometimes means being able to laugh at yourself!

I'm very proud of how I can take chaos and arrange it to make sense. Being a conductor is second nature for me, and when faced with a complex situation involving many factors, I enjoy managing all of the variables, aligning and realigning them until I'm sure I have arranged them in the most productive configuration possible. There is nothing special about what I do; I'm just trying to figure out the best way to get things done. But others, lacking this trait, have been in awe of my ability.

"How can you keep so many things in your head at once?" they will ask. "How can you stay so flexible and so willing to shelf well-laid plans in favor of something just discovered?" I cannot imagine behaving in any other way, it's who I am, a shining example of effective flexibility, whether it's changing travel schedules at the last minute because a better fare popped up, or mulling over just the right combination of people and resources to accomplish a new project. From the mundane to the complex, I'm always in search of the perfect configuration. Of course, I am at my best in dynamic situations, confronted with the unexpected.

Some complain that plans devised with such care are absolved from adjustments, and others take refuge in the historical procedures that would prevent any modification. I don't do either; instead, I tend to jump into the confusion, devising new options, hunting for new paths of least resistance, while figuring out new partnerships—because, after all, there might just be a better way.

I was designed to be a maximizer, someone who takes full advantage of every moment and opportunity. Transforming strengths, whether my own or someone else's, fascinates me. Like a diver after pearls, I search them out, watching for the tell-tale signs of strength. A glimpse of untutored excellence, rapid learning, a skill mastered without recourse to steps—all these are clues that a strength may be in play. And having found a strength, I feel compelled to nurture it, refine it, and stretch it toward excellence. I will polish the pearl until it shines. This natural sorting of strengths means that others might see me as discriminating. I choose to spend time with people who appreciate my particular strengths. Likewise, I am attracted to others who seem to have found and cultivated their own strengths, avoiding those who want to fix me and make me well rounded. I've put in the work to fix me and don't want to spend my life bemoaning what I lack. Rather, I want to capitalize on the gifts and strengths with which I am blessed. It's more fun. It's more productive. And, counterintuitively, it is more demanding. After years of hard work on myself, and having such an understanding of who I am as a person, accumulating my knowledge of self has become the equivalent to a diploma one would receive for their matriculation through the School of Life.

Acknowledgements

TO THE LOVER of my soul, the one who assigned me purpose long before I could even speak. God, you are worthy of all the praise! You are truly the source of my strength.

To my son, you, my love, gave me the fuel to persevere and reach for more so that I could provide better for you! More education, better neighborhoods or better sports teams. A better me for a better you was my desire as I raised you. You deserve nothing less and I did my best to give you that. At times I failed and other times I succeeded. I love you with all I have and thank you for understanding that we grew up together.

To my siblings, Candie, John, Joe, George and Lorraine I know that parts of my story are also yours. I hope that the words shared in this book don't retraumatize you. Understanding that our parents lived in a far different world than we live in today. The need to survive the many challenges that they faced is pale in comparison to what we are faced with now and that's including a global pandemic.

I hope you find a sincere understanding and peace of mind knowing that God is faithful and will heal any wounds that we have as a result of our parents' choices.

To my big brother, Charles aka Charlie, (I always like to say we share the same mother and father) and my baby brother, Marvin.

Growing up together, it was always Charlene, Charlie and Marvin. We had parties of three for almost every birthday celebration. Charlie, you taught me how to love unconditionally and Marvin, you showed me how to love intentionally. Our bond is epic and one that has no boundaries. Thank you for always supporting and encouraging me to do more.

To the "Book Squad" for this project, Melica Blige, Tameka Johnson, Tjien Johnston, Heather Nelson, Melissa Skinner, and Assata Michelle Thomas. Each of you are an immeasurable blessing to me; not just with this project but in so many ways. Thank you for all of the candid conversations, sound advice, for listening and allowing me to vent and process my emotions throughout this whole journey. To my best friend, Terri A Miller, you are one of my biggest cheerleaders. You make me feel like a rockstar all of the time. You have been my truest forever friend. To my sister-friend, Katrina Milton, you have been my sounding board for all things social work since we first met. I love and appreciate your support and enthusiasm..

Dr. Mary Patton, you saw in me more than I ever believed in myself. Thank you for being a healer, mentor, motivator and friend. Kelly Mobley of Kelly Kaptures: Your eye and ability to create a vibe is spectacular! DerMekka Dodson: My makeup artist, your talent is amazing. Melissa Falissano: My stylist, we have worked together for over 20 years. You have dressed, encouraged and prayed for me and I love you and your family dearly. Kamile Kuntz, Book Cover and Robert Brown, Website Design, thank you for accepting the assignment and delivering more than I could have imagined. Julie Peterson, you consistently provided logistics whenever I needed direction with this project and were a constant encourager and true mentor. Thank you Soror, you are the epitome of sisterhood. To my editor k. Edward, thank you for helping me to write my story. As a graduate student, I was once told that my writing was so bad that it made the reader sick to their stomach! I was intentional in my prayer request for an editor. I needed someone that would instinctively meet me where I was and not distort my confidence in this process. I was unaware, when our paths crossed, what God's intentions were but over time His perfect plan was revealed,—YOU were the answer to my very specific prayer. You guided me through this journey from the very beginning. Your love and patience was exactly what I needed to complete this project. You allowed me to be vulnerable without judgment or shame. You not only taught and challenged me, but you also encouraged me when I needed it most. You are truly gifted. Get ready, there are more authors like me who need your brilliance. Donica, thank you for lending me your eyes at the last hour. Love and appreciate our sisterhood Soror! To my finisher, Melicia Morgan, thank you! You patiently waited from the start for me to say I'm done! To the man in the chair sitting in the dark, your words encouraged me to be powerful without fear. I cannot fully convey the gratitude I have for the candid conversations we shared. Our paths crossing was certainly divine intervention.

P.S. I extend a special thank you to my siblings Loraine, Charlie, Candie and sister-cousin Linda for being my historians for this project. I know that our conversations may have triggered some emotions. I want you to know how thankful I am for your willingness to help me with the facts as I worked on this project. Xoxox

Resource Guide: Building Resilience

DISCLAIMER: THIS TEXT is not meant to be a clinical guide, but a resource for mental health professionals, laypeople, clergy, teachers, childcare providers, foster care parents, emergency room providers, and others in various organizations, to be deemed a framework when working with individuals that may have had a history of trauma.

Understanding Trauma and its Impact

Trauma is defined as an event, series of events, or set of circumstances that is experienced by an individual as physically or emotionally harmful or life-threatening and that has lasting adverse effects. Traumatic events range from one-time incidences to experiences that are chronic and even generational.

How Trauma Affects the Mind

Trauma can provoke a wide array of emotional and cognitive reactions. Depending on an individual's personal characteristics, in the context of their environmental and cultural background, these reactions can include confusion, exhaustion, sadness, anxiety, dissociation, and physical arousal. Trauma can also profoundly shape an individual's worldview perception of personal safety and interpersonal relationships.

How Trauma Affects the Body

Traumatic events can deeply affect an individual's physiology, so far as to actually change the chemical makeup of the brain, increasing the risk for developing certain physical ailments.

Experiencing trauma at any point of development can profoundly alter the brain's structure and makeup. Healthy human brain development is based on environmental input, being shaped by the experiences of the individual's life. Additionally, the brain consists of complex neural networks that interact with each other constantly. When one section of the brain is impacted, it is likely to affect other areas of the brain. If one's life experiences include chronic trauma, the brain's neural networks can restructure and affect areas of the brain that impact the emotional and physical regulation of the body. Trauma also affects the body's autonomic nervous system. This system initiates a series of brain and body responses when a person is threatened, which trigger survival instincts (such as the flight or fight response). Typically, after the threat has passed, the autonomic nervous system shifts the body's survival reaction to a calmer, more restorative mode. For those who have experienced traumatic stress, this response system can become dysregulated, leading to an overreaction (such as becoming hypervigilant) or underreaction (feeling depression and dissociation).

Trauma Categories

- **Acute trauma** refers to a one-time event, such as an earthquake, fire, assault, or car accident.
- **Chronic trauma** refers to traumatic experiences that are repeated and prolonged, such as ongoing exposure to family or community violence, chronic bullying, or a long-term medical issue.
- **Complex trauma** refers to the pervasive impact of exposure to multiple, simultaneous, or prolonged traumatic events. The feelings and behaviors associated with complex trauma can produce a domino effect and facilitate subsequent or repeated trauma. Examples include abuse and neglect within families, witnessing domestic violence or experiencing

other forms of violence or adversity without adequate adult support.

- **Traumatic stress** that induces the flight/fight/freeze response. Unlike typical stress, traumatic stress includes intense physical and emotional responses that can have a lasting impact.
- **Re-traumatization** is the recurrence of traumatic stress symptoms upon exposure to multiple traumatic events. Also includes re-experiencing traumatic stress symptoms when a new situation is similar to prior trauma.
- **Secondary or vicarious trauma:** experiencing trauma-related psychological and physical symptoms in response to helping or empathizing with others who have experienced traumatic events. This is very common among helping professionals working with trauma survivors.

Because of the potentially long-lasting negative impact of trauma on physical and mental health, new ways to address a person's history of trauma have drawn the attention of healthcare policymakers and providers across the country. Exposure to abuse, neglect, discrimination, violence and other adverse experiences increase a person's lifelong potential for serious health problems and engaging in health-risk behaviors, as documented by the landmark Adverse Childhood Experiences (ACE) study.

Let's look at how cross-sections of populations intersect with each other during a crisis.

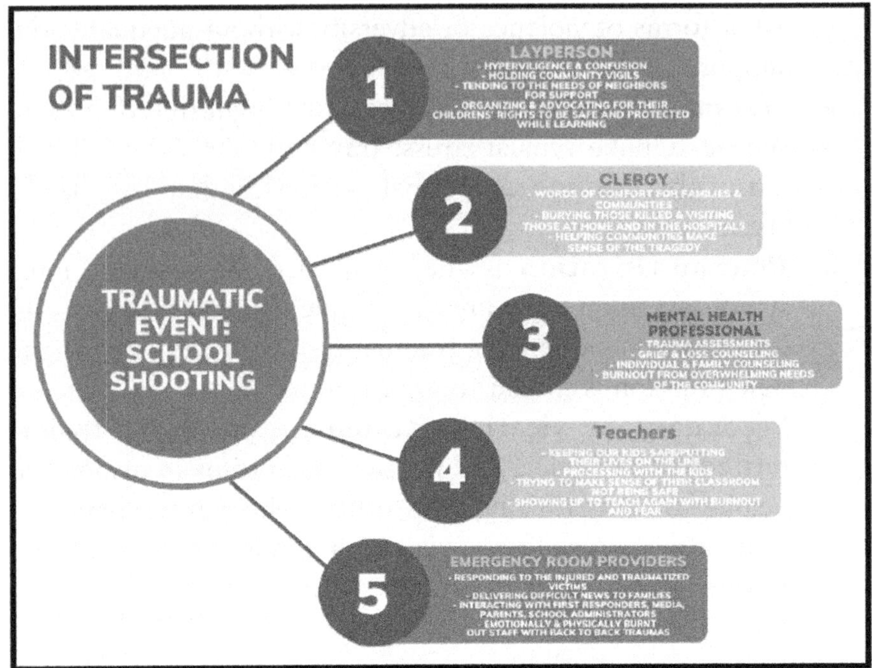

What Are ACEs

The Centers for Disease Control and Prevention (CDC) and Kaiser Permanente conducted the first ACE study from 1995 to 1997 and asked more than 17,000 adults about childhood experiences including emotional, physical, and sexual abuse; neglect; and household challenges of parental separation, substance abuse, incarceration, violence, and mental illness. Nearly two-thirds of participants noted at least one ACE and more than one in five noted three or more. Researchers identified a link between ACE exposure and a higher likelihood of negative health and behavioral outcomes later in life, such as heart disease, diabetes, and premature death.

Adverse childhood experiences, or ACEs, are potentially traumatic events that occur in childhood (0–17 years). For example, experiencing violence, abuse, or neglect, witnessing violence in the home or community, or having a family member attempt or die by suicide are just a few adverse experiences children may endure.

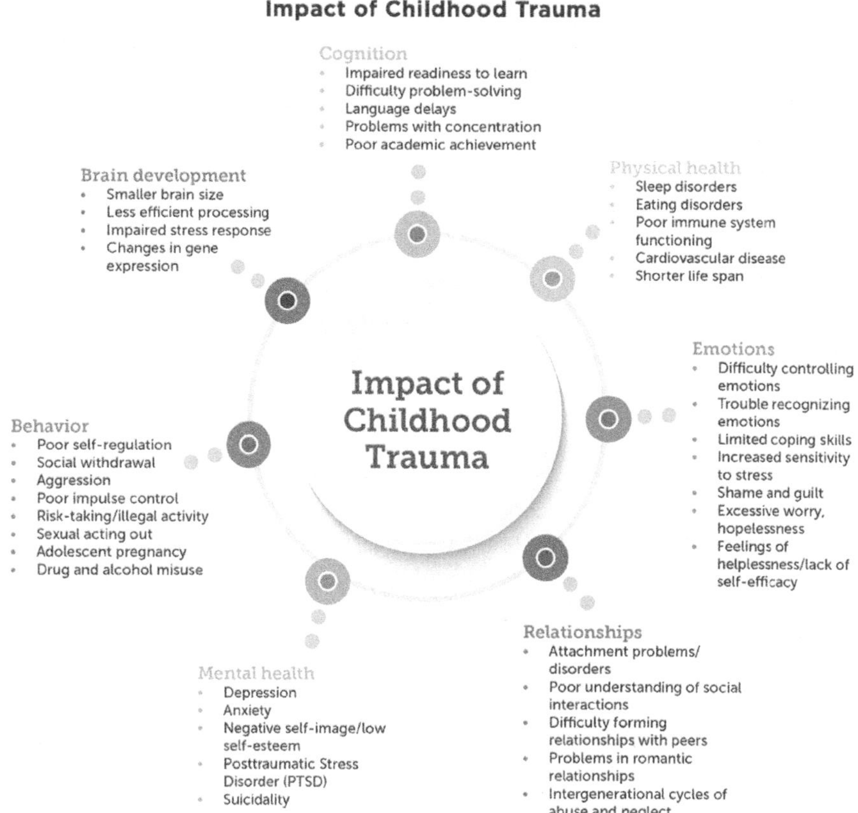

credit goes to Kelly Kaptures

Also included are aspects of the child's environment that can undermine their sense of safety, stability, and bonding, such as growing up in a household with substance use problems, mental health issues, or instability due to parental separation or household members being incarcerated. ACEs are linked to chronic health problems, mental illness, and substance use problems in adolescence and adulthood. ACEs can also negatively impact education, job opportunities, and earning potential, but can be prevented.

Please note the examples listed in this text are not a complete list of adverse experiences. Many other traumatic experiences could impact an individual's health and wellbeing.

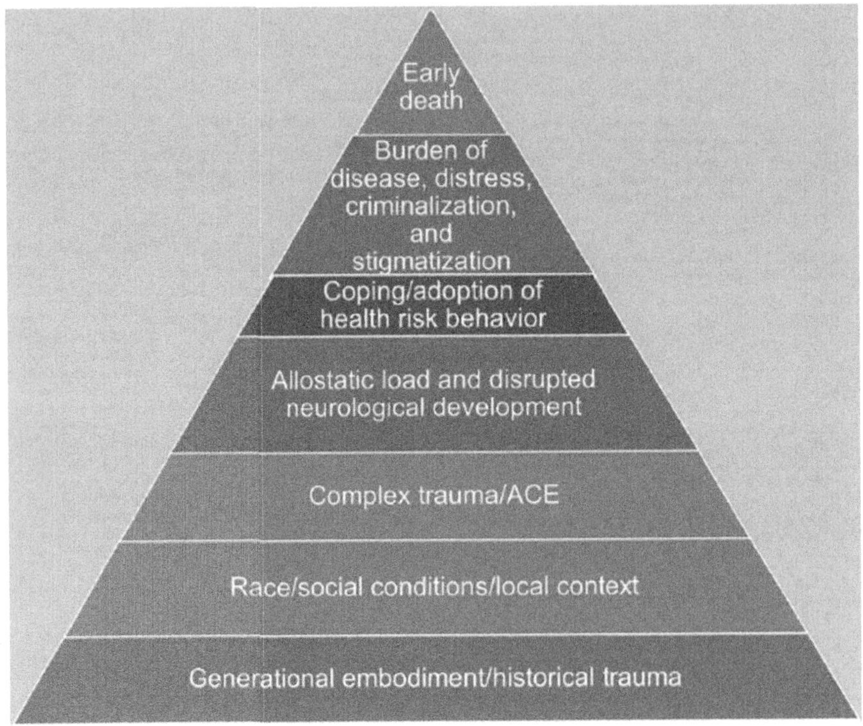

Source: Centers for Disease Control and Prevention. (2016). Violence prevention: *The ACE pyramid* https://www.cdc.gov/violenceprevention/acestudy/about.html

When thinking about trauma or adverse trauma one must first understand and recognize that there is a common denominator that we all experience, yet our response to the adverse trauma whether individually or collectively will differ. The global pandemic of 2020–22 was one thing we all had in common in addition to the fear of the unknown, as there appeared to be a lack of transparency specifically related to the origin of the virus and how it could be transmitted. By January 2020 there were small conversations about COVID in the news, but it was not *major* news until March when information began flowing from every media outlet. There was no place one could turn and not be bombarded by what then became an overload of COVID reporting. No matter who you spoke to or what media outlet you watched there were no answers that made any logical sense to the massive number of people dying daily. In the first six months, over 200,000 people had died from COVID-19. At one point, health officials said those who had underlying health problems were at a greater risk of dying from the virus, which attacked at will. And, if that wasn't enough COVID did not discriminate against gender or race and began taking the lives of healthy, active men and women. Hospitals had no beds, nursing homes had patients dying with no staff to support them because they too, had fallen victim to the monster, COVID-19.

TIP: Understanding Historical Trauma: Historical trauma, also known as generational trauma, refers to cumulative emotional and psychological pain experienced by a specific cultural, racial, or ethnic group over a lifespan or across generations of people en masse. The enslavement and oppression of African Americans in the U.S., the forced migration and colonization of Native Americans in the U.S., and the genocide of Jewish populations during the Holocaust have all had psychological and physical health impacts on a population and have resulted in individuals being hesitant to enter systems of care that have historically oppressed these populations. Systemic racism can't be fixed with a town hall meeting, nor can trust be restored when considering how the government over time has failed the community in such drastic ways that have left the bridge of communication, trust, and even mutual respect shattered.[9]

In 1932, the United States Public Health Service and the Center for Disease Control and Prevention conducted what has and will forever be the most unethical experiment and research during the 1900s, which led to the genocide of the African American male. The study was called the "Tuskegee Study of Untreated Syphilis in the Negro Male," in which the government took 400-plus Black men from the rural south, most of whom were poor and illiterate, and made them test subjects with the knowledge that there was no treatment. That wouldn't be so bad, as we understand research is required for the creation of innovative measures designed to advance new and effective remedies; however, in 1947 when penicillin became the primary source of treatment for syphilis, the CDC withheld the medication from those men who'd taken part in the study, leaving hundreds of men, women, and children to become infected with syphilis or die from the disease. After 40 years a special council was established to investigate the horrific tragedy, and many were to blame. Ethics 101 according to Charlene: Informed consent to use these men for this study had not been legally obtained; the truth regarding life-threatening side effects had been withheld, and in the eyes of African Americans, the Government had got away with murder in 1947, ultimately creating skepticism as it would relate to the current health epidemic of COVID-19. As a result, members of the African American community did not trust the government, and did not jump on board when the news of a vaccine for COVID-19 became "magically" available; especially since there were mixed conversations about the vaccine's origin, which created more resentment in an already damaged relationship.

There were also theorists making claims around the time and circumstances of the virus's development, which also caused many to suspect its authenticity. Severe acute respiratory syndrome (SARS) and Middle East respiratory syndrome (MERS) are two diseases caused by coronavirus, juxtaposing their relationship to another virus that causes COVID-19. The CDC began working on a vaccine in 2003, and again in 2012 during a SARS outbreak which impacted a few States within the United States, and a few other countries; whereas, with COVID-19 a global pandemic ensued. What we didn't know during the 2020 outbreak was that the virus had disappeared in 2017, making it difficult to determine the potential success of a vaccination. A few years later another form of the SARS virus was discovered, unlike anything ever seen, as it did not respond to treatments previously used to mitigate SARS. It was all scientific mumbo jumbo that I still don't fully understand, but it allowed researchers to complete what they had started back in 2003, making the vaccine for COVID-19 readily available and effective in lessening the impact of the coronavirus.

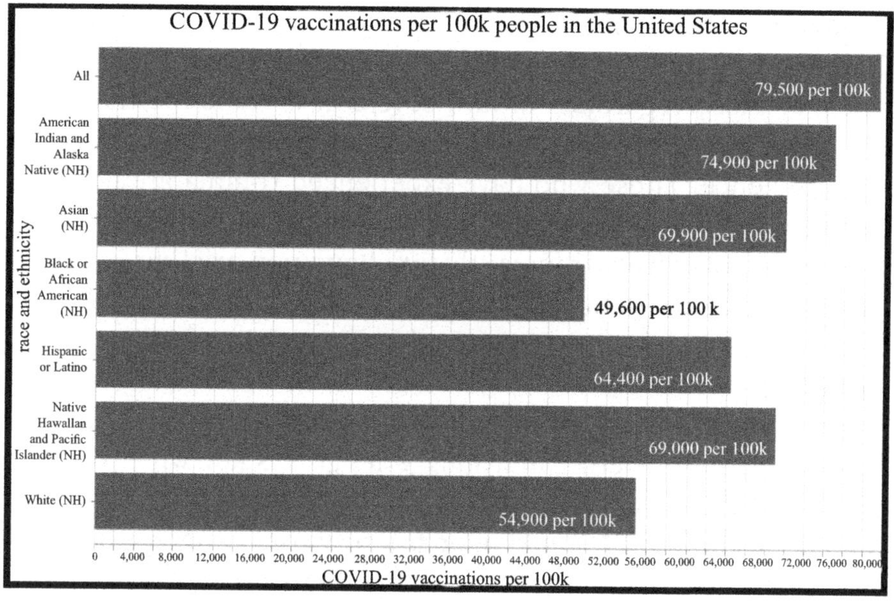

Sources: CDC COVID-19 Vaccination Demographics in the United States, National (updated October 2022), American Community Survey 5-year estimates (updated 2019), and American Community Survey 5-year estimates from 2010, U.S. Territories (updated 2010).

The experience of trauma is widespread in society. Research suggests that 70% of adults will experience at least one traumatic event in their lifetime. While not all traumatic experiences will result in a trauma disorder (such as post-traumatic stress disorder), trauma remains a risk factor for nearly all behavioral health and substance use disorders. In fact, over 90% of clients receiving public behavioral health services have experienced some type of trauma. Resilience is the ability to rise above or "bounce back" from adversity. It is a trait that can be found in individuals, but it can also be broadly applied to families, communities, and organizations. The recognition that people can overcome traumatic stress by building resilience is a central tenet of the trauma-informed care framework.[10]

Rather than assuming that one is either born resilient or not, trauma-informed care recognizes that everyone can become resilient. For most, regardless of how severe or chronic the traumatic experience, the immediate or enduring effects of trauma are met with resilience. Those who have experienced trauma are not condemned to a life of hopelessness and helplessness—people can—and do—recover from trauma. By building upon existing strengths and applying new tools for coping, resilience is a skill that can be fostered.[11]

Supporting Resilience

Advocating and fostering individual strengths is key when working with trauma survivors. This essential strategy is important for several reasons. It helps to build upon the survivors' existing skills, and promotes courage and resolve, allowing them to see themselves as resourceful and resilient. A trauma-informed approach enhances the individual's resolve and celebrates their ability to adapt as well as acquire new coping skills.

Cultural Factors of Resilience

Characteristics of an individual's cultural, racial, or ethnic background can often nurture resilience. Research suggests that having a strong connection to one's cultural background, community, and traditions is not only vital to the individual, but can also impact and influence future generations.

Culture can have a very strong influence on the perception of trauma for the individual, and in some cases can create negative outcomes (e.g., a sexual assault survivor could be ostracized from their community). It is imperative as you work with individuals to be cognizant of the cultural background and the meaning of the trauma for the individual. The risk of re-traumatizing the individual, or implications for harm, should be considered, as well as an understanding of the risk that it may present.

Steps to Building Resilience

Social Support

Being connected to social networks, whether they are through school, faith-based communities, work, or other networks, helps strengthen an individual's stress response.

Getting Back to Normal

Having lived through a global pandemic, I don't know if getting back to normalcy is as easy as it reads. However, being able to resume a daily routine and experience success completing tasks can help in creating a sense of normality. It is important to understand that structure and routine is paramount in decreasing the stress of trauma after one experiences a traumatic event.

Purpose

If the survivor of trauma can glean or provide a meaningful reason as to why the traumatic event occurred, and is able to ascertain the silver lining in the event, a positive takeaway can be achieved. This mindset will facilitate the healing process and empower the survivor.

Supporting Resilience in Others

Being trauma-informed and supportive to others is everyone's responsibility: employers, teachers, medical professionals, emergency professionals, and anyone who engages with others. Empathy and understanding of others helps the individual not be re-victimized and promotes healthy outcomes. For example, employers who provide avenues to practice self-care and other resilience-building tactics are better positioned to support staff and reduce employee turnover and burnout in highly stressed positions.

Strategies to Promote Resilience in Others

Building resilience in others is providing the survivor with the needed tools to overcome traumatic events. It's important in the survivor's journey to heal that they believe there can be recovery from their pain, and that the support needed to ascertain the "silver lining" is available.

Peer support helps prevent feelings of isolation, as statistics show that many survivors who have experienced traumatic events will self-medicate and have the potential to abuse alcohol and engage in other maladaptive behavior in an effort to mask the pain they may be experiencing, which is why it is important to provide a space where trauma survivors can open up and share the emotional distresses associated with the trauma. Ideally this would be achieved in support group settings.

Education and Training

Most people would think that a lack of education and experience will prevent them from supporting a survivor on their road to recovery; however, that is not the case. In order to be trauma-informed one would only need to be aware of their own sense of empathy, in that we all have experienced something—a dissolving marriage, chronic illness or even eviction—that has created a sense of loss and hopelessness. To be trauma-informed as a layperson, remembering what it was that you felt, what you needed in the moment and how you overcame will allow you to better engage and be more empathetic as you work with those who have experienced trauma.

Understanding Triggers

Triggers are signals that act as signs of possible danger based on historical traumatic experiences, and are relative to a person and the trauma. No two triggers are the same, and their effects are equally distinctive, as a scent can be a trigger for one person and a sound for another. Triggers can also lead to emotional, physiological, and behavioral responses that arise in the process of survival (e.g., sounds, smells, sights, and even touch). Understanding an individual's triggers will better equip you in navigating conversation and allow you to be more understanding.

Maintaining Balance

Maintaining a healthy life-work balance is important when working with individuals who have experienced trauma, because if you can't be good to yourself how can you be any good to anyone else? Practicing self-care results in good mental and physical health and should be done often; frequent exercise and proper rest, as well as developing solid coping skills and making healthy life choices, can help individuals better manage stress.

The following tips will help in establishing and maintaining a healthy balance.

1. **You don't have to be perfect.** A lot of overachievers develop perfectionist tendencies at a young age when demands on their time are limited to school, hobbies, and maybe an after-school job. It's okay to not get everything done. You are doing your best.
2. **Exercise and meditate.** Exercise is an effective stress reducer. It pumps feel-good endorphins through your body while lifting your mood and bringing clarity to your thinking process.
3. **Make a schedule for rest**. Resting doesn't always have to equate to sleeping, but scheduling time to relax can be

beneficial. Intentionally do things that give you comfort, peace, health, and happiness. Make a deliberate effort to prioritize your needs.

4. **Start small. Build from there.** Living in a microwave world makes this one hard. You don't have to conquer the entire mountain. Chunk it out one step or bite at a time. Start small and build momentum through small victories.
5. **Find a support system**. Find the people in your life who build you up and support you, who add value to your life and inspire you to be a better version of yourself. Try to avoid people who add or create more stress for you. Remember that stress affects you physically, so within reason, consider phasing out those who might be causing your stress or imbalance.
6. **Take control and say no**. Often people say yes to others because there might be an unreasonable pressure to immediately please people. It is important to consider your current list of responsibilities. Take time to think about what you can reasonably complete and try to alleviate adding extra stress by learning how to say NO.

Endnotes

1 https://www.psychologicalscience.org/publications/observer/obsonline/how-mother-child-separation-causes-neurobiological-vulnerability-into-adulthood.html?pdf=true

2 https://www.complextrauma.org/

3 https://www.childtrends.org/publications/how-to-implement-trauma-informed-care-to-build-resilience-to-childhood-trauma

4 Adams, C. M. (2006). The Consequences of Witnessing Family Violence on Children and Implications for Family Counselors. The Family Journal, 14(4), 334–341. https://doi.org/10.1177/1066480706290342

5 Bartlett, J. D., & Steber, K. (2019). How to implement trauma-informed care to build resilience to childhood trauma. trauma, 9(10).

6 New Living Translation

7 https://jacksonhealth.org/blog/2018-01-25-five-reasons-sexual-assault/

8 Hollowood, T. (2017, September 4). Why Can Childhood Sexual Abuse Lead to Promiscuity?, HealthyPlace. Retrieved on 2023, April 10 from https://www.healthyplace.com/blogs/traumaptsdblog/2017/09/childhood-sexual-abuse-ptsd-and-promiscuity

9 Pumariega AJ, Jo Y, Beck B, Rahmani M. Trauma and US Minority Children and Youth. Curr Psychiatry Rep. 2022 Apr;24(4):285-295. doi: 10.1007/s11920-022-01336-1. Epub 2022 Mar 14. PMID: 35286562; PMCID: PMC8918907.

10 Article: Building Resilience Relias.com

11 Article: Building Resilience Relias.com

Mental Health Helplines And Resource Referrals

988 Suicide and Crisis Lifeline:
24/7 for crisis counseling and resource referrals
Call 988

The Trevor Project Lifeline
Crisis counseling hotline for LB+GBTQ youth
Call 1-866-488-7386
www.thetrevorproject.org/get-help

Trans Lifeline
Peer support hotline for trans people
Call 1-877-5658860
www.translifeline.org

Call BlackLine
Peer support hotline for Black, Brown and Indigenous people
Call or text 1-800-604-5841
www.callblackline.com

National Alliance on Mental Illness Helpline
Peer support line and resource referrals
Call 1-800-950-6264
www.nami.org/help

211
Resource referrals and information about mental health, food, and housing support services
Call 211
www.211.org

"What stands between a disrespected African American and the source of disrespect is almost four hundred years of history, four centuries of being the targets of humiliation and abuse. A history of racial conflict, inequality and contempt culminates in a moment that few people not of the culture could comprehend, let alone predict"

Dr. Joy DeGruy

Made in the USA
Middletown, DE
15 September 2023